CHILDHOOD is the basis of the future, and I believe in religious instruction for American children. The future of the nation cannot be trusted to the children unless their education includes their spiritual development. It is time, therefore, that we give our attention to the religious instruction of the children of America, not in the spirit of intolerance, nor to emphasize distinctions or controversy between creeds or beliefs, but to extend religious teaching to all in such form that conscience is developed and duty to one's neighbor and to God is understood and fulfilled.

WARREN G. HARDING,
President of the United States.

The Abingdon Religious Education Texts
David G. Downey, General Editor
WEEK-DAY SCHOOL SERIES.   GEORGE HERBERT BETTS, Editor

The New Program of Religious Education

BY

GEORGE HERBERT BETTS

THE ABINGDON PRESS
NEW YORK   CINCINNATI

Copyright, 1921, by
GEORGE HERBERT BETTS
All Rights Reserved

Printed in the United States of America

First Edition Printed October, 1921
Reprinted January, 1922; March, 1922; September, 1923

CONTENTS

What shall the church do to be saved?—Saving the
body and saving the soul—No saved church in a lost
world—*Practical temper of the times:* New standards of
efficiency in social institutions—New demands upon
the church—The church cannot escape evaluation—
Tests to be applied to the church: Results which cannot
be measured—The test of clear aims—The test of the
influence exerted by the church—The test of right
methods—*A pressing question:* The church facing the
test—Issues at stake.

Conflict of opinion usually not to be deplored—
Conflict may block action—The conservative and the
progressive—Religious education and evangelism—
The viewpoint of religious education: Work upon
childhood the most fruitful enterprise of the church—
Conservation, with reclamation a last resort—Religion can be taught—The demands of religious education—*The evangelistic viewpoint:* Fear that religious
education will substitute training for divine influence
—Conversion as the aim of church activity—*Contrasting the two points of view:* Detailed parallel comparison of respective claims—Conclusion.

Difficulties arising out of failure to define education
and religion—*Changing concepts of education:* Changes
in meaning undergone by this term—Fading of the
disciplinary from the concept of education—The modern meaning of education—This concept applied to

CONTENTS

FOREWORD

THIS little volume is an attempt to define the aims of religious education and show its place in the scheme of the church's activities.

In every new movement there is a time of indifference followed by a period of misunderstanding, confusion of thought, working at cross purposes; then acceptance. On the matter of religious education the Protestant Church is just now passing over from the first of these stages to the second; indifference and complacency are giving way to interest and concern, yet the new program is far from practical realization or even full approval. Much conflict of opinion and uncertainty still exists.

Some see in the movement for religious education the dawn of the millennium, others think it a valuable adjunct to the church's present program, while still others are frankly skeptical over the whole project. The new term "religious education" means very different things to different people who use it. To some it is an effective tool for evangelism; to others it is a means of escape from necessity for the evangelistic method. Not a few see in this movement a great new social and spiritual force; but many say it is another fad and will soon be heard no more.

These and similar questions are discussed in the present volume from the point of view of one who frankly believes in the possibilities of religious education when that term is rightly conceived. The changing concepts as to the function of the church are noted; the causes underlying the conflicting currents of opinion concerning the

9

place of religious education are analyzed; religious education is itself defined; the interrelations of the educational and the evangelistic method are set forth; an explanation is sought for the church's relative neglect of religious education; changes which would follow a full acceptance of religious education as a major enterprise are outlined; and a sketch is made of the program required to make religious education fulfill its purpose in the modern church.

It should be understood that the positions taken, while presented with deep conviction, are intended rather to open than to close the discussion. The writer believes that the topics considered are among the most vital and crucial confronting the Christian Church to-day. In his presentation he hopes to bring these problems anew to the studious attention of church leaders whatever their denomination, position, or authority, to the end that the church may effectively place the religious education of youth at the forefront of its enterprises.

CHAPTER I

CHANGING CONCEPTS

WHAT shall the church do to be saved? This is not mere sensationalism. The startling question is gravely being asked by serious men to whom the life of the church means more than life itself. What! Bluntly ask such a question of an institution whose avowed business it is to save others? Throw it like a bludgeon at an organization that has outlived oppression and tyranny and to-day numbers its adherents in hundreds of millions?

Let us get this straight. No intelligent person believes that the Christian Church is in the least danger of going out of existence as an institution. Its corporate life is entirely secure, for as long as civilized men maintain an organized society so long will they have an organized religion, that is, a church. The question goes much deeper than this. It turns on the *kind* of church we shall have.

It will be remembered that in Jean Valjean's dream when he was fighting a great moral battle with himself one called out to him, "Jean Valjean, you are dead." "I am not dead, I am alive," he answered. "No, you are dead; *you have killed your soul!*" came back the reply.

Not the body of the church, but its soul is in danger. What shall the church do to save its soul, its spiritual dynamic, its constructive influence for righteousness which alone gives it the right or the power to assume moral leadership among social institutions and to claim the respect of men? What shall the church do to save the self-respect which comes only from the consciousness of the fulfillment of obligation and the realization of destiny? What part will it play in the reorganization of human values now going on? Will it be able to take the offensive in the struggle against selfishness, greed, and the many forms of iniquity that have gained sway, or will its fight be a defensive one, satisfied with victories already won and with ground already gained? Will the church aggressively face forward and outward ready to meet new times and conditions, or will it turn its gaze inward and backward in enervating contemplation of its glory and traditions? These are the questions that many earnest souls are to-day anxiously asking.

Those who mocked said, "He saved others, himself he cannot save." Like its Founder, the church cannot save itself except through saving others. It is unthinkable that a church can save itself in a lost world. For a church exists only to serve, and when effective service ceases the church no longer lives; its soul is dead. Only as it goes out into the world of men and affairs, out where the tides of life are strong and where evil abounds, out where human need is greatest, and there sets a lamp to the feet that go astray and throws a light upon the pathway that leads to a sure goal can the church be saved. Nor perhaps does it greatly matter whether a church that would not be willing and able to do these things should be saved or not.

PRACTICAL TEMPER OF THE TIMES

In a new and peculiar sense the church is to-day on trial at the bar of social judgment in the Christian world. While it is no longer unjustly held responsible for not having prevented the war, it is rightly held to account for taking a leading part in the spiritual regeneration of a disorganized world. This is a large contract, and the way in which it meets this challenge will go far to determine the place the church is to occupy among social and spiritual forces for the generations that lie immediately ahead.

It will not do to answer the challenge in terms of past achievement. That the church has many glorious pages (along with some dark ones) in its history all who know its past will gladly agree. Nor will it serve to appeal to a loyalty founded on sentiment alone. For the temper of these times is preeminently practical. The lessons of the past half dozen years have taken deep hold on the social mind. We demand results. We seem determined to quit guessing or assuming all along the line and go to finding out—finding out whether results are commensurate with claims and costs in every social institution.

The necessity for this attitude has been forcibly thrust upon us. For example, we recently found that twenty-five per cent of our young men were disqualified for effective military service because of physical disabilities; so we rightly go to our public-school system and our national, State, and municipal health authorities and ask them what is the matter and what they are going to do about it. We discover that we have eight or ten million illiterate Americans among our population; naturally, we inquire what is wrong with our boasted free, universal, compulsory education and what remedy it proposes. To our astonishment the war uncovers a considerable block of people living under the American flag and receiving the benefit of its protection who shamelessly refuse loyalty and allegiance to our country when the supreme test comes; and we at once demand why the agencies responsible for educating, Americanizing, and socializing our adopted citizens do not do their work.

And this practical attitude, or scientific spirit, if you

will call it that, extends to the functions of the church as well. We are bent on carrying out very literally the injunction to "prove all things." We are willing to "hold fast to that which is good," but we want to be very sure that it will not turn to dust and ashes if we are to hold to it. Hence it is that standards which have been accepted for centuries are being ruthlessly examined, and methods which have been employed for generations are required to defend their position. Tradition is no longer held in supreme regard just as tradition, nor dogma because it is dogma. Nothing is secure that cannot prove its right to a place in the scheme of things as they are or as they ought to be. *Measure, evaluate, test*—these are the watchwords of the present-day spirit, and they will inevitably be applied to the church and its methods in common with other forms of social enterprise.

TESTS TO BE APPLIED TO THE CHURCH

In so far as the results of the church's enterprises and activities are measurable at all (many of them are not measurable), they should be measured by the same standards that would apply to other social institutions. The church can claim, and desires to claim, no exemptions because it is a church. Yet the church can be most fairly judged and most fruitfully criticized by its friends —those who believe in it and its mission. The best friend of the church, however, is not the one who accords it warm but indiscriminating praise, ignoring its weaknesses and errors. In the end we gain little from the physician who, instead of correctly diagnosing our ailment, would lull us into a false sense of security and well-being when a disease has fastened itself upon us. One of the great needs of the church to-day is fearless, friendly, clear-headed constructive evaluation and criticism; not for the purpose of finding fault but with a view to clearer definition of aims and more effective methods.

What are the tests by which the church is to be judged as to its efficiency and promise—by which it is to judge itself? Probably we shall not all agree upon the details of these tests, but upon the broader principles involved there should be little room for controversy; and space will here permit the statement of only the most general principles.

The church's aim. Has the church a clearly defined aim, certain definite and attainable ends set as the goal of its effort? Does it know exactly what it is trying to do, so that it may determine whether it is succeeding or failing in its enterprises? And are the goals sought sufficiently concrete and real, so that it may be surely known when they have been attained or missed? Does the church know the true function of a church in a social process such as that of the present, so it may judge whether this function is being fulfilled?

It has been estimated that in the world war an average of one thousand shots were required to hit a man. And this in spite of the many marvelously refined range-finding devices and niceties of mechanism for aiming the guns. One is bewildered by the thought of how many shots would have been required to hit a man if there had been no definite aiming and no specific objectives! Has the church improved and efficient range-finding devices? Has it sufficiently well-defined objectives? Does it know what it is aiming at?

No one will dare to be dogmatic in answering the question about the church's concept of its aim—unless he chances to belong to an infallible (!) church. Yet there are many evidences of confusion in thinking or of failure to think at all about the true aim and function of the church.

To some the church is a glorious heritage handed down by saints and martyrs, a precious charge to be zealously guarded and defended and kept unspotted from contact with an unfriendly world.

To others it is a means and a symbol of personal salvation, a convenient instrument for a preliminary separating of the sheep from the goats, a secure fold in which the elect can rest and possess a foretaste of the bliss that awaits them in the world to come.

To still others the church is a social refuge, a kind of club to which we go on Sundays and listen to a sermon, perhaps worship, and hear attractive music and see and be seen.

Or it is so many buildings, more or less impressive, usually with spires, often with bells, with organs and altars and pulpits and pews, with doors always open on Sundays and commonly closed most of the rest of the week. But a church must be more than any or all of these things.

To a promising and growing nucleus the church is a *means* and not an *end;* a cooperative association of those who believe in the way of living set forth by Jesus, both for themselves and the world at large; an instrument for the joining of our common effort in making practically effective in the social life of to-day the spirit and message of its Founder; a going concern, which must be keenly sensitive to each changing spiritual problem of its generation, ready at any moment to adapt method and program to meet the needs of those it serves; a democracy of opportunity for spiritual growth, the development of character and the offering of unselfish service for the betterment of our generation.

All these and various other concepts of the true nature and mission of the church exist in the minds of the mass of its constituents. There is great need of a clear, convincing dominant note of enlightenment and conviction sounded by recognized leaders of the great rank and file on this important question of what the church really is and what it is for.

The simple fact is that in spite of much zealous and violent suppression of error; in spite of many battles royal over conflicting theologies; in spite of subtly defended claims to the possession of infallible truth concerning the church; in spite of recent centuries of freedom for laboratory experiment in the Christian religion; and (strangest of all anomalies!) in spite of the surpassingly simple and clear message of the gospel, the church seems still to be uncertain of its true aim and mission. Most of all is it uncertain as to the best methods for carrying out its aims. The inevitable result of this confusion is uncertainty, indifference, lack of confidence, energy working at cross-purposes, and consequent loss of power and failure of achievement. The church believes it is on the way but is not wholly sure whither it is going or the best way to take to reach its destination.

The influence of the church. Is the program of the church succeeding? Does it attract to itself not only increasing numbers of people, but an increasing *proportion* of the population? Is the growth of the church satisfactory? Does its prestige increase? Is its voice accepted as a voice of authority when it speaks on moral and religious questions? Are its own constituents trained and intelligent, loyal to the church and informed as to its enterprises? Do they readily and efficiently participate in the program of the church's activities, freely rendering service through its agencies?

Here again the answer must be relative, for there has been far from failure in most of these items. Yet the showing in some of them gives thoughtful friends of the church grave concern and suggests the necessity for careful consideration in order to save from actual disaster.

For example, the church has unquestionably suffered a considerable loss of prestige in the last generation or two. It has lost both relatively and actually in esteem and authority. Nor will it do to ascribe this attitude of the public to a growing worldliness for which the church is not to be held accountable. There are many evidences that the disaffection is not against *religion*, but, rather, against the church as an instrument of religion. Further, if there has been an actual decline in responsiveness to religion, *the church must be held responsible for this condition,* for it is the business of the church so to meet its problem and adjust itself to human needs that widespread irreligion does not develop in its constituency.

A natural result of loss of prestige on the part of the church is failure to attract membership. No complete and dependable statistics on church affiliations in the United States exist. The following figures are, however, probably approximately correct.[1]

Protestants in the United States. 24,354,000
Catholics, Jews and other non-Protestants. . 21,076,000
Not members of any church. 58,110,000

Thus it is seen that fifty-six per cent of our population are not members of any church. The proportion is even more unfavorable than appears on the face, since many whose names are on church rolls are practically never found in church buildings. Perhaps even a worse feature is that there are some twenty-seven million children and

[1] From Inter-Church World Survey, p. 208.

youth (under twenty-five years of age) in the United States who are receiving no religious instruction and are practically without direct religious contacts. Probably three children and youth out of four under eighteen years of age are receiving no religious instruction. But the most discouraging factor of all is that this unfortunate condition has been gradually growing worse instead of better. Just at present there are some signs of a slightly turning tide, but the change is not yet marked.

As an inevitable corollary of this showing, there is a widespread and increasing ignorance of the Bible and the Christian religion among all classes of our people. And this spiritual illiteracy occurs at a time when general education and enlightenment are rapidly advancing.

Even children and youth reared in church homes and, more astounding still, those whose names are on the roll of the Sunday school often show little knowledge of the Bible and of the fundamentals of the Christian religion. Of the church and its program, even of the particular church in which membership is held, little is known by the average church member. The church cannot build safely on the foundation of a constituency who do not go to church, and do not know their Bibles or the foundations of the Christian faith.

Some will raise the cry of alarmist at this point and call attention to the fact that the church has had a long history, has withstood many attacks and much hardship and persecution, and is stronger to-day than ever before.

As was said in the earlier part of this discussion none need be alarmed concerning the continued existence of the church as an institution. The question is not the saving of the body of the church but the salvation of its soul and of the *world*. The Christian Church has now had three centuries of absolute freedom in this country.

Yet to-day we find it occupying but a comparatively small part of its rightful territory, its membership, if not relatively on the decrease, for the last two decades at least not making marked advance, its constituency not deeply interested in the written or the preached Word, its children growing up in varying degrees of ignorance of religious matters, its spiritual dynamic unable to stem the tide of moral laxness and lowered ethical standards now sweeping over the nation.

Now, these facts call for explanation. There is failure, at least relative failure, somewhere. Is Jesus Christ a failure? Is the message and program that he gave unequal to the task laid upon it in this century? Or is the church failing—failing through its program and its method to give the system set forth by Jesus a fair trial?

The church should not rest until this question is satisfactorily answered and the challenge fairly met.

WHAT SHALL THE CHURCH DO TO BE SAVED?

What shall the church do to be saved? The most immediate and possibly the most important thing it can do is to welcome and accept wholeheartedly the challenge that comes to it in this modern demand for practical results. For whether with its consent or without it, this test *will be applied*, is even now being applied and judgment will be rendered.

If the church is willing to face the issue squarely; if it recognizes that it will not serve to continue on the basis of its present efficiency; if it will earnestly go at the business of finding out its own weaknesses and seeking to remedy them; if it will concern itself with discovering how to fulfill its function in the rather unsatisfactory world of to-day instead of expending its energies in defending its traditions (though many of its traditions will grow stronger with sharp testing); if in self-forgetfulness it will seek to serve rather than to be served—then the church shall be saved and, saving itself, will save the spiritual values of civilization. But if the church is not wise enough or great enough to do these things, . . .

CHAPTER II

CONFLICTING CURRENTS

CONFLICT of opinion is not to be deplored in the church any more than in any other social organization; for truth oftenest emerges out of free discussion, and opposing policies or principles are best tested in competitive struggle against each other. Yet the contest is seldom an even one, for the presupposition is always in favor of that which is. Tradition gives an advantage to principles long accepted and to policies already in operation. The burden of proof is rightly upon those who would make a change. The conservative has only to "sit tight," the progressive must make his case. Especially is this true in the field of religion which, from its very nature, is and should be conservative.

Perhaps the opening sentence should be modified to say that conflict of opinion and the waging of discussion are not to be deplored unless the conflict and the discussion absorb interest and dissipate energies that should go into action. It is possible, even in the church, for opposing camps to be so busy confounding each other that the common enemy goes unscathed. It sometimes happens that lack of understanding and mutual suspicion of sections within an organization render impossible the team work required for success and so defeat the purpose of the enterprise.

Such a situation of misunderstanding and strain exists in some degree in the Protestant Church to-day. Two sets of principles and policies are increasingly in conflict. And until this conflict is settled and concert of effort and action rendered possible the work of the church cannot go forward successfully.

THE VIEWPOINT OF RELIGIOUS EDUCATION

On the one hand we have a new group, the advocates of *religious education*. Right or wrong, they are the progressives of the church on this particular issue, for they counsel a radical change of method and a marked shifting of emphasis by the church in its program of activities. They have through their plans and enterprises even given us, within the last decade, the new term in our religious vocabulary, "religious education." To them also we owe another term, the "church school."

The promoters of religious education are not timid. They feel sure of their ground. They tell us that *the primary obligation and opportunity of the church, standing out ahead of all other obligations and opportunities whatsoever, is the religious education of its childhood and youth.* True, they do not make religious education the *only* function of the church. They recognize the fact that the church must minister to many social interests and needs; the church must be an evangelist to reclaim the wayward, a philanthropist to help the needy, an educator to war against ignorance, a missionary to less favored peoples, a reformer setting up standards of righteousness.

Yet the advocates of religious education insist that the religious nurture and training of childhood and youth is a greater and more fundamental thing than the reclaiming through evangelistic effort of adults, or than the promotion of philanthropic enterprises, or than the waging of social reforms. These believers in religious education do not advise that the church relax its efforts at reclamatory evangelism, that it lay aside its philan-

23

thropic work, that it quit the field of social reform, or, indeed, that it lay down any other good work. But they do insist that first things shall come first, and they are very confident what the first things are. So they demand that the church adopt a new program with religious education in capital letters at the head of the list of its enterprises, conceiving this as the foundation of all other church activities or programs. Contrary to the assertion that "the great need of the church is new zeal," these leaders say that it needs first of all *new method*, and that out of this new zeal will come.

Pursuant to this policy the religious educationists undertake to apply the scientific principles of general education to the teaching of religion. They insist that religion *can be taught* just as other things can be taught. They tell us that the same powers of mind are used in unfolding the religious consciousness, apprehending religious knowledge, developing religious emotions, and arriving at religious decisions that apply in other forms of experience; and that therefore the genetic psychology of religion must govern the treatment accorded the child in his religious life.

On the practical side these advocates of religious education advise that more of the child's education time shall be given to education in religion. They ask public school authorities to surrender a portion of the school time for instruction in religion to be conducted under the auspices of the church. Where time cannot be had from this source they ask parents to send their children to religious classes before or after the public-school day, or on Saturdays. They invite children to attend the classes in religion, either taking a part of their public school time or a part of their play time for this extra work.

Having planned for the children, these educators address the teachers of religion and officers in the church schools. They are asked to attend training schools, or to organize study classes, or to follow a prescribed course of professional reading in order that they may apply the scientific principles and methods of education to their teaching or supervision.

Next they approach the churches themselves and ask them for a greatly increased budget to employ paid teachers of religion for week-day classes and directors of religious education and in order to buy new educational equipment and build classrooms in which the teaching of religion may go on. They come to the church editors and publishers and ask for new curriculum materials.

THE EVANGELISTIC VIEWPOINT

On the other hand is another and at present a much larger group, the conservatives of the church, who are complacent over the present system, or who are indifferent to, mildly opposed to, or frankly skeptical about the whole movement for "religious education." Another fad, they say, which will have its little run and then die out as so many other fads have done before, while the grand old church goes on forever. Besides, they add, have we not the Sunday school with its millions of children, and its thousands of devoted teachers and officers who give themselves gladly to the religious training of children? And does not an astonishingly large proportion of our church membership come from the Sunday school? Religious education! What would you have? Are not our children now receiving the religious instruction they require?

Nor are many of the conservative group without suspicion that there is grave danger that "religious education" will end by substituting *education* for *religion*. A representative of this group, addressing a Sunday-school convention, asserts, "The Sunday school trains the *heart*, while 'religious education' trains only the *head*. Now, religion is more a matter of the heart than the head. Therefore the safest thing is to support the good old-fashioned Sunday school and let 'religious education' alone." Another, this time one who holds one of the highest offices in the gift of the church says, "'Religious education' is all right in its way, but what we need is to get back to the good old-fashioned revivals and the good old-fashioned religion." Another conservative church official, addressing a group of young ministers, advises them, "Give less time to 'religious education' so called and more time to preaching the effects of sin." Still another traditionist leader, speaking to an assembly of religious workers, advocates religious education, but concludes his address with the advice, "If a child can go but to the Sunday school or to the public preaching service on Sunday, by all odds take him to the latter." In other words, not teaching, after all, but preaching is what the child requires.

What the child needs, says this group, is just what any person needs, to be "soundly converted." He needs to "accept Christ" and become a Christian. What we ought to desire for the church, they tell us, is not more "religious education" but more evangelism in order to bring men (and children!) to a sense of their sin, to repentance, to divine acceptance and to regeneration. Said one distinguished evangelist: "If I had a million dollars to spend for religion, I would use nine hundred and ninety-nine thousand, nine hundred and ninety-nine dollars and ninety-nine cents for evangelism; and then I *might* use the remaining one cent for religious education."

True, the conservative group does not ignore religious education, as conducted in the typical Sunday school. Indeed, it is this group that has built the Sunday school up to its present status. But by religious education in this sense they do not mean just what the advocates of religious education mean. They look upon the Sunday school not primarily as *educational* but *evangelistic* in function. Its primary purpose from their point of view is to prepare the child for conversion and lead him to membership in the church. When these ends are accomplished the great objective of the Sunday school has, as they conceive it, been accomplished.

CONTRASTING THE TWO POINTS OF VIEW

These deep and far-reaching differences of position and policy are partly, but only partly, removable by a fuller understanding, each of the position of the other. Though it is probable that the progressive, the religious educationist, understands the position of the conservative, the traditionalist, better than the position of the former is understood by the latter. This is for the simple reason that present religious educational leaders have for the most part grown up under the older traditions and have separated themselves from the traditionalist policy from conviction, and hence know what that position is.

The differences between the points of view of these two groups are chiefly the differences of two contrasting methods which may for our present purpose be called the *educational* method and the *evangelistic* method. A parallel comparison of the two methods will serve to bring out their respective characteristics.

The Educational Point of View	*The Evangelistic Point of View*
1. The child is at the beginning right with God (the explicit statement of the Methodist Episcopal Church and the view accepted by most evangelical Christians and certain others.)	1. Whatever the status of the child at the beginning he, nevertheless, because of inherent sinful tendencies, requires reclamation through conversion.
2. The aim of the religious educational process is to lead to a gradual and continuous unfoldment of the spiritual nature of the child such as results from a perpetual acceptance of the Christian way from the beginning. This acceptance is at first unconscious, being directed by nurture and instruction, and leads to the formation of religious habits, interests, and ideals.	2. The aim of the Sunday school is to prepare the child for the day when he will become "converted" and "accept Christ." In this connection and to this end he is to be instructed in the Bible and religion.
3. The child whose religious consciousness develops normally will naturally and inevitably come to a time or to times of personal acceptance of the Christian way (that is of Christ), thus adopting by conscious choice the relationship and obligations	3. When the person has once been "converted" the great work of saving grace is completed. The person concerned is now a "Christian," is "saved," a member of the "fold." Growth from this on may be desirable, but, after all, the great thing has been ac-

28

The Educational Point of View

The Evangelistic Point of View

into which he has gradually been led from earliest childhood. This personal commitment of the child-Christian is both natural and desirable. It should not, however, be called "conversion," in the sense of reclamation from spiritual indifference, hostility, or evil.

complished, in the one cataclysmic act of being converted.

4. Religious experience, like any other form of experience, is a gradual growth, a process of evolution in the life. Hence spiritual growth obeys the same laws that govern in other phases of the life and in other forms of human experience. A full, rich religious consciousness and sense of personal acceptance and spiritual well-being may therefore be attained by the normal growth process providing right nurture and guidance are provided.

4. The entering into religious experience and right relationships with God is accomplished at the time of "conversion," the occasion usually being accompanied by a feeling of emotional stress, a sense of guilt, repentance, submission, and acceptance by Christ.

5. Accepting the position of the child's right status with God, but conscious of native tendencies in the

5. While possibly accepting for purposes of theological discussion the theory of the child's right

The Educational Point of View	*The Evangelistic Point of View*
original nature which will, if unchecked, lead to evil, the religious educational process strives to keep the original bond with the Divine unbroken, so that reclamation will never be required. The program of the church is, therefore, to be, first of all, one of conservation of childhood rather than reclamation of adults.	status with God, there is, nevertheless, a tacit assumption in favor of "original sin" or a "depraved nature" which for all practical purposes makes it necessary for the church to make its program largely one of reclamation.
6. It is freely admitted that the religious education program cannot be made to work one hundred per cent effectively. Through lack of human wisdom, through spiritual indifference in the home, through abnormalities in child nature and through failure to put the religious educational program into effect, the church will still require a well-planned and well-executed program of reclamatory evangelism. The importance and necessity of this salvaging process will naturally grow less as the religious educational program is more fully de-	6. Religious education is welcomed provided it act as an aid to evangelism, but decidedly not if it seeks to render evangelism unnecessary. Evangelism is the primary enterprise of the church.

The Educational Point of View	*The Evangelistic Point of View*
veloped. Evangelism is rightly the last resort of the church instead of its primary enterprise; a confession of failure or weakness at some point in the religious training of childhood and youth.	
7. The most promising point of attack and the chief strategic opportunity of the church is with childhood. The church should therefore make *teaching* in the classroom its primary function and chief method of gaining adherents and training them to Christian character and service.	7. The preaching of the Word is the great mission of the church. The children should regularly attend the preaching service, though the preaching will be directed to adults.

On the personal side the members of these two groups work in entire harmony and friendship, with sincere good will and the spirit of helpfulness. Both are moved equally to promote the cause of Christianity and the church. Each takes its positions from deep conviction (though not always equally reasoned or tested) of their validity and the ultimate success of the methods employed. Each is actuated by praiseworthy motives and usually by commendable zeal. Still they differ quite radically, and at some points in such a way as to hamper the success of the great enterprise of the church.

Who is right? How shall the radical differences between these two points of view be reconciled? Shall the church depend chiefly upon the evangelistic method and center its efforts on adults as it has done in the past, only putting more zeal into the world? Or shall it change its method, stressing first of all the making of Christians by the gradual processes of education, and employing the evangelistic method as a supplement in order to salvage that remnant who escape the educational method or fail to respond to it? No more important question than this now confronts the church. Its further consideration will occupy the remaining pages of this discussion.

CHAPTER III
WHAT IS RELIGIOUS EDUCATION

No small part of the indifference or hostility to religious education comes from a failure fully to understand just what is meant by one or both of the terms "education" and "religion" as used by the religious educator.

CHANGING CONCEPTS OF EDUCATION

The word "education" does not mean what it formerly did. It is, of course, obvious that any word means just what those who use it put into it as meaning; the form of the word may remain the same but its content changes from age to age.

There was a time when education meant only the ability of a slave or underling to read an occasional letter or legal form for his master; or to write at his dictation some brief communication of social or business nature. Education stood for so little in the thought of the times that the man of affairs would have none of it, leaving that to those he could command or hire.

At a later time education was defined chiefly as the ability to read in the original tongue in which they were written certain great literary classics and to discourse learnedly about them; manifestly such education was for the few, and not for the many. Following the Lutheran Reformation education meant the power to read the Scriptures, each for himself, translated into his own native tongue. In John Locke's time, we are told, education meant the training to be an English gentleman— that is, the preparation to spend graciously and gracefully what someone else had provided.

For some two hundred years prior to the opening of the twentieth century education was conceived as *the discipline of the mind*, the training of the intellect, the sharpening of the wits, teaching to think, reason, discriminate. The particular kind of knowledge gained was not nearly so important as the exercise the mind obtained in the operation. So that the matter was difficult enough and sufficiently logical to afford a rigid intellectual gymnastic nothing further was required.

In this *"disciplinary"* type of education the feeling and volitional side of life was neglected. The attitudes, the emotions, the appreciations, the interests were entirely secondary. Similarly, the instincts were overlooked, the tendency to expression was ignored, the motives leading to self-activity were left out of account; knowledge was "imparted" to a passive recipient. There was no thought of carrying instruction directly over into action, and so into habit and character.

There are many earnest people, especially those accustomed to the older regime, who still look upon education as an affair of the head only, the heart (that is, the motives) being left entirely out. To them education concerns itself solely with the intellect, storing it with knowledge and training it in the processes of thinking. Such persons say: "This may be all right for general education, but not for religion; for religion touches the heart even more than the head; it is a matter of affection, love, loyalty, devotion, allegiance, righteousness, the indwelling of the divine spirit in the human heart. And such fruits as these cannot come by any mere training of the *mind*. It is the *soul* we seek to save in religion."

Precisely. And that is what education undertakes to do in the modern sense of education. Education deals, as we understand the term now, not with any one department of life, but with the whole of it. It trains the intellect not more than the affections, the appreciations, the loyalties, the devotions, the aspirations. It reaches down to the springs of action, influences conduct, forms character, guides achievement, shapes destiny. Education trains the heart as much as the head, it reaches to the will, helping form its decisions, and provides motives for self-direction. It appeals to the conscience, stimulates self-respect, creates regard for others, and sets up the law of allegiance to the common good. It deals with the *whole* person and not just a part.

More specifically, the aim of education has to-day become very concrete and definite. It looks out upon life, the life of to-day, and seeks to discover what that life demands of the individual as a successful participant in the social process, attaining the fullest development and satisfaction for himself and contributing most to the welfare of his generation. What life at its fullest and best demands of the individual, that education seeks to supply.

There are three things which life demands of every normal person:

1. *Usable knowledge;* either (1) to function in the gaining of other knowledge, or (2) to serve as a guide to action, conduct, character, service to others.

2. *Right attitudes;* that is, fruitful interests, high ideals, worthy loyalties, fine appreciations, noble loves and hates, the spirit of artistry in work and achievement, the inclination to service, such standards of value as give a true philosophy of life.

3. *Skills in living;* the power and the will to carry the knowledge gained and the attitudes developed directly over into daily life and conduct, thus transforming them into action, building them into habit, character, achievement.

This, in brief outline, is a definition of the purpose of education as we conceive it in the modern sense. It supplies the *knowledge* necessary to intelligent living in the world to-day. It undertakes to stimulate, organize, and put into action the great underlying *motives* that control action and conduct. It seeks to make knowledge and motive find expression at once in *applied skills* to be developed and used in the everyday run of daily living. No element or factor of the life is to be omitted from the educational ideal, no fundamental need is to be neglected, no power, physical, mental, social, or spiritual is to be left out. The public school is to be chiefly responsible for the *physical*, the *mental*, and the *social*. The church must be responsible for the *spiritual*, the religious. These four factors, rightly developed to coordinate with each other, will give us a complete system of education for our children, for they provide for the four-fold nature of man and meet the demands which life puts upon the individual.

Now, if education were the narrow thing that many still conceive it to be; if it reached only the "head," thus training the intellect but leaving the "heart," the great source of motives, untouched; if it did not concern itself to see that its teachings were carried over into action and so into habit and character—if these things were true about *education*, then *religious* education could mean little or nothing, and every person who believes in the spiritual outcome of life would be justified in being skeptical as to its value for the church. But these things are *not* true of education to-day. Education has entered, in the last two decades, upon a new era of meaning and of service.

This is education in the newer sense, the education which gives vital meaning to the term when we say "religious education." It is this new meaning of education which renders this proposition true: *"What you would have in the life of the church you must first put into its schools."*

CHANGING CONCEPTS OF RELIGION

Religion not less than education has recently been undergoing a re-definition of meaning and aims, which makes it all the more imperative that the educational method shall be employed. It is yet too early in the process of readjustment now going on to make a full interpretation of the changes in religious concepts under way, but some of the more outstanding changes of concept are clear.

Religion is becoming more of a dynamic *function* in life, both the life of the individual and the life of society. Even before the war the pragmatic temper was growing, and men were coming to judge the quality of religion less by the creed or the order of the ritual than by the way personal morals and action and conduct in social relations squared with the great basic demands for righteousness, justice, and decency as understood by the common conscience regardless of theology or creed. The effect of the war was, of course, greatly to accentuate and stabilize this movement.

While this age has too keen a sense for psychological values to fail to recognize the importance of *belief* in religion, its demand for practical values is so strong that it is concerned primarily for the great *fundamental* beliefs held for the most part in common by all Christian groups —belief in the Fatherhood of God and his goodness to men; in the value of righteousness and the curse of sin; in the way of living set forth by Jesus of Nazareth. Theological niceties and ecclesiastical distinctions have a small and decreasing interest for the great mass of persons to-day who are interested in religion. They ask for a *rule of life*, not a complicated statement of creed or a particular form of worship. Religion is to be a mode of living, a type of character, a system of conduct, and not a compartment of the life shut off from the remainder, a section of experience attended to on Sundays and then locked away until the next Sunday comes about. It is to be conceived as an active, working principle starting from the very center of the affections, desires, ideals, motives, and thence working outward to the periphery of the life, giving color and tone and spiritual quality to all other phases of experience. What does this is *religion*, and what fails to do this cannot qualify as religion under the increasingly practical concept of it.

Religion is becoming increasingly social in its nature and its aims. The older theology made of it a very individual matter between one person and his Maker. The great goal was a personal salvation, a "getting to heaven," a keeping free from the snares and entanglements of the "world."

Such a concept is not sufficient for a "social century," however. Individual salvation is not lost sight of, but a merely selfish personal salvation with great masses of society not included in the salvation is becoming unthinkable. "Serving God" is coming in a new and more pregnant sense to mean to serve his needy children. Salvation of the soul is increasingly conceived to be linked up with saving the body, the health, the habits, the ideals, the interests—indeed, the whole range of the being. Life is more and more being looked upon as a unity in which one part cannot be "saved" while the remainder is neglected and ignored. The "world" is being interpreted in a new sense as the environment in which our lives must be lived, and this "world" may itself be transformed to make it a favorable medium in which to cultivate a soul. Indeed, it seems that it may become necessary to quit speaking of "the world, the flesh, and the devil" in the same breath as natural correlates.

The view of religion that gives it this practical applied trend, that makes it a function of the whole life, that connects it all seven days of the week with individual and social conduct, that makes it an integral part of personality and character—this vastly fruitful and dynamic concept of religion carries with it the inevitable corollary that religion is a matter of *growth and development*, an inseparable part of a growing and expanding life experience, no more to be attained in a day than any other aspect of the nature. This is equivalent to saying that religion is best and most effectively to be attained gradually as a part of nurture and education; for only in that way can it be built in with other aspects of experience and so made to be a natural expression of the inner self.

THE MEANING OF RELIGIOUS EDUCATION

What, then, is religious education? What does it seek to do and how does it go at it?

First, on the negative side, what religious education does *not* do. It does not, as some have feared, seek to substitute any process of mere *training* for the spiritual element in religion. It does not leave the divine factor out, offering therefor a fund of information *about* religion. It does not deny the fact and power of conversion acting on a life that has drifted from its spiritual relationships and needs to recover them. It does not aim at an ethical system alone, unsupported by the religious motive. In short, it does not omit any agency commonly used by the church to stimulate and develop the religious consciousness, with this exception; religious education *seeks to save the need for* a reclamatory conversion, and in its stead substitute a gradual and natural spiritual growth in the course of which, *at the proper age, the child will make a personal decision and acceptance of the Christian way in which he has from the beginning been led.*

On the positive side, religious education takes the child, endowed through his original nature as he is with capacities both for evil and good, and seeks to stimulate the good and suppress the bad, using for this purpose religious instruction, nurture, and guidance. Far from discarding or disregarding the supernatural factor, the working of the "grace of God," religious education believes so thoroughly in this factor that its great aim is to keep the bond between the child and his heavenly Father from ever being weakened or broken. It seeks so to train the child and stimulate and guide his spiritual development that this divine grace shall have constant access to the heart and life, a sustaining, organizing, upbuilding power acting continuously upon the soul, rather than expecting it to reclaim a sin-sick soul which has lost its way.

Religious education believes in evolution, the evolution of the soul. It pins its faith to a slow and steady growth of the religious consciousness going on unbroken from the earliest years to the end of life. It accepts the position that in his spiritual development the child employs the same powers of mind and heart and will that are used in other avenues of experience and that the law that will hold in one realm of experience will hold in another.

Building upon this position religious education utilizes the principles and methods that have been proved successful in other phases of education, adapting them to the particular aims and needs of religion. It believes that what you would have in the life of a people you must first of all put into the schools; and, believing this, undertakes to put religion into the (church) schools in such an effective way that religious concepts, religious attitudes, and religious activities shall become an integral part of the child's nature, a part of his inner self, naturally and continuously expressed in each day's life as it is lived in the common round of responsibilities and duties.

No one claims that religious education is a panacea. There is no magic in it any more than in any other kind of education. It uses the method of the tortoise rather than the method of the hare. It is not a perfected system, nor indeed ever can be. It will never produce one hundred per cent of results. Some children, owing to mistakes and weaknesses in the religious educational system itself, or because of negative influences operating on the child from some other phase of his environment, will fail to respond, as some fail to respond in the public-school system. Some will never be brought under its influence at all, either through the lack of appeal of the system or the indifference of their parents or some other cause.

We will remember that about one person out of twelve above ten years of age in this country is unable to read or write—and this in spite of what is probably one of the best systems of general education in the world. There will as a matter of course continue to be a certain percentage of spiritual illiterates, no matter how perfectly we undertake to work out our religious education program. The church will always require its other agencies—its pulpit, its evangelism, its reform programs, and many other enterprises. But these should rest on a solid foundation of religious education, which alone can give the church an intelligent, loyal, spiritually equipped body of workers to carry on its program.

CHAPTER IV

RELIGION THROUGH EDUCATION

ONE of the most striking social phenomena of the present day is a world-wide renaissance in education. Many years ago von Humboldt said, "What you would have in the life of a nation you must first put into its schools." Acting on this advice, Germany put militarism into her schools and through them made the World War. While the war was still in progress every great nation involved in the struggle was working toward the perfecting of plans to use public education as a chief instrument of rehabilitation the moment the time was ripe. Within a year after the armistice was signed England had placed on her statute books the most far-reaching educational measure the empire has ever seen. France is doing her best to a more effective system of national education, as are Germany, Japan, China, and the United States.

What does it mean? Simply that education has been newly discovered. The state has come to see that whatever of national efficiency, of public health, of patriotism, of thrift, of character we would have in our nation we must put into its schools so that it will become a part of the life and experience of our children from earliest childhood to maturity. What thus grows up with the individual becomes an integral part of him, a permanent possession in his life, and so in the social aggregate crystallizes finally into national type and character.

Does this principle hold for religion? Are the things of the Spirit subject to the same laws of growth and development that apply to other aspects of the nature? May a full, rich religious consciousness be attained by a process of gradual evolution in the individual as it is in the race? Can one *grow* in grace? Can the child be so guided, his habits so shaped, his desires so trained, his affections so formed, his sense of God's presence and meaning in the world and in his own life so cultivated that he will never know a moment of conscious separation from the Divine, and that when he has arrived at the age of personal choice and self-direction he will naturally and inevitably choose to follow in the Way? Is it true that what we want of *religion* in the life of our people we must first put into our (church) schools? *Can religion be taught?*

THE TESTIMONY OF PERSONAL EXPERIENCE

Thousands upon thousands of devout Christians can testify to the truth of this statement: *Religion can be taught.* The writer has asked several hundred persons to answer the following questions:

1. Can you point to *some particular time or occasion* when you began the Christian life, in the act commonly known as *conversion*, meaning by this *a turning from a state of spiritual coldness or indifference or rebellion* to a recognition of the claims of Christ upon you and a consciousness of his acceptance of you? Or,

2. Did you *grow so gradually* into your present religious status that you *cannot point to any particular time or occasion* when you were *converted* and began the Christian life?

3. In either case, have you had times or experiences of *personal commitment, re-decision* or *reconsecration of* your life to Christ? If so, how often and at about what age?

These questions are shaped to bring the issue sharply between entering upon a consciously religious life suddenly by *conversion* and gradually by *growth*. Also, to indicate whether it is usual, no matter which has been the initial process, for the individual to pass through experiences of personal decision, commitment, and reconsecration.

Those to whom the questions were given were persons markedly interested in religion, and who presumably had a religious consciousness and experience of clear and definite sort. Nearly half of them were ministers and seminary students preparing for the ministry. The remainder were church-school teachers taking work in training classes, and university students in departments of religious education preparing for special lines of religious service. Care was taken to make sure that all thoroughly understood exactly what was meant by each question. To encourage full and frank statements no names were to be signed to the answers.

About forty-five per cent of the entire number answered that they had experienced definite conversion. About fifty-five said that they could fix no time or place of conversion, but from their earliest recollection had counted themselves as Christians, having been brought up in Christian homes and under religious instruction. Nearly all of both groups testified to passing through from one to several times of personal decision or affirmation, or of special consecration or definite recommitment to the Christian life. The method of entering upon the religious experience, whether by conversion or by the normal growth process seemed to make no difference on this point, thus indicating that such personal affirmation or re-commitment experiences are normal and to be expected.

Of course, the significance of these answers does **not** lie in the particular percentages belonging to each group. This will vary among different groups.[1] The point in question was whether it is possible for normal, average persons to develop a vital religious consciousness and a sufficient belief in and concern for religion to be willing to enter definitely into its service without having passed through the experience called conversion. Another form of the question is whether it is possible so to train, instruct, and nurture a child in religion that he will develop a strong, fine Christian character, never having known estrangement from God nor having to be reclaimed from a life of spiritual hostility or indifference. The indisputable reply to these questions is *Yes*. It is beyond question true that *a full, rich, vital religious consciousness can be developed by a process of normal growth without the necessity of conversion or any emotional upheaval.*[2] Experience proves that *religion can be taught*—not the experience alone of the few hundreds of persons concerned in this inquiry, but the experience also of many of the world's brightest lights of Christian leadership, together with that of hosts of their followers. None may doubt that the grace of God is able to save a soul through conversion; and none may doubt either that it is able to save that soul from the need for conversion (that is, of reclamation)! To have to reclaim by conversion a soul that should never have known separation from the divine is the supreme tragedy.

THE TESTIMONY OF PSYCHOLOGY

Psychology joins with common sense and with mod-

---

[1] Compare the well-known studies of Starbuck and Coe.

[2] *Conversion* throughout this discussion is used to mean a *reclamation* and the turning from a life of spiritual indifference or rebellion to a life of conscious and purposed harmony with God. Acts of *re-consecration, re-decision* or *re-affirmation* are not called conversion, and should not be.

ern theology in not imputing to the child any inherited load of guilt bound to him as a child of Adam. Indeed psychology is not concerned about "original sin," but about *original nature*.

Let us take the point of view of the psychologist and consider the nature and tendencies of the child. The child is the product and culmination of an age-long evolution, he bears the impress of a limitless past. The blood of a million generations flows through his veins and the deeds of countless ages of life stir in his brain. He is the product of myriad centuries of conflict and battle. And nature has garnered up the fruits of all these racial experiences through which every new being born into the world has come, and handed them on to this child in the form of instincts, impulses, and various forms of innate tendencies.

These native tendencies form the great basic "drives" of human nature. They are the starting point for most lines of action possessed in common by the race. Most of these instinctive drives were at one stage of the racial past necessary and good. Possibly some of them were always bad. Not all that were once necessary and good are so in this day of civilization, though most, perhaps all, instincts and impulses play some good part in the child's development or in his later life. Even these that are now good, however, can be made evil of by wrong use or overindulgence.

Thus it comes about that the child's original nature supplies him with an equipment of tendencies and powers which form the groundwork of his life but which need direction. Some of these instinctive tendencies need to be encouraged, trained, educated, set at work as motivating forces back of action, conduct, achievement, and character. Others of them need to be suppressed altogether, or at least held strictly in check by being balanced by others of an opposite kind.

The child's heritage from the past of his race, his original nature, the psychologist would call it, gives him, therefore, almost limitless capacities both for good and for evil. He comes into the world a child of God; he has committed no wrong, his moral record is clear. But he has had planted in his nature seeds which, if allowed to grow and bear fruit, will yield a harvest of sin and evil. *In that case he will ultimately need conversion* to cleanse his soul of this spiritual harvest of evil. On the other hand he has other seeds planted in his nature which, if carefully nurtured from the first and brought to fruition, will crowd out or keep down the seeds of evil and will bear a harvest of spiritual good-will and responsiveness to God and fellow man. *In this case no conversion will be required*, for there will be no growth of spiritual coldness or rebellion or purposed evil from which to be reclaimed.

It is not only possible, therefore, but entirely natural for the child to grow gradually into a full religious experience. It is the great business of education, of *religious education*, to see that he does this very thing. For this is by far the best and the safest way.

Attaining religion through the processes of growth and development, that is, through response to religious nurture and training during childhood and youth, is the best way for many reasons. First of all, this is the only method by which religious ideals, habits, and actions can be made so much an integral part of the nature that they become second nature, no more to be put off or laid aside in times of stress or temptation than personality itself. It is a well-known biological law that only the *constants* in an environment, those factors that are continuous in their contact with the organism, are able to modify organic structure and function. Those factors that are only occasional or intermittent, that appear only temporarily at certain stages in the life history of the individual, produce no fundamental and lasting change.

The same principle holds in the spiritual realm. It is those influences that enter the life early and that are constant in their pressure on the expanding soul that are able profoundly to determine its quality and shape the course of its development. Only as religious concepts are built in with the growing body of the child's general fund of knowledge and thought will they become a part of his mental structure and be a dependable factor in shaping decision and action. Only as religious feeling and appreciation develop along with other phases of feeling and appreciation will they operate normally as a part of the motive forces of the life. Only as religious acts and deeds become a part of the general structure of habits by being interwoven with them as they grow and strengthen from earliest childhood will religion become an integral part of daily life and experience.

Not without cause is the church concerned over the tendency of its members to make religion a formal, incidental matter—a something added on as a supplement or afterthought, rather than a something built in, the core of the life. It is lamented that there is so often a broad gap between profession and practice, between creed and deed, between what the head accepts and the conduct expresses. So many persons have a tendency to make their life upon the plan of water-tight compartments, with religion in the Sunday compartment and pretty much left out of all the rest of the week. The remedy? There is one simple formula which will come nearer solving this fatal weakness in our practice of the Christian religion than any other: *Make religion an integral part of the child's education throughout the whole period of his plastic development. Build religious concepts, attitudes, and habits into the expanding life from the first, so that they may become an inseparable part of its structure.*

True, the adult may become converted. His life may be transformed by the strange alchemy of divine power working in it. But no life grown to maturity without contact with religion can ever make religious thoughts, feelings, and actions as natural, inevitable, and effective a part of his experience as they would have been had they been built into the growing life from the first. For such a person religious concepts and values must always in some degree be attached to an already built mental structure, an addition that was not in the original plan when the structure was building. *Introducing religion into an adult life that has never known it is like trying to graft a new shoot on an old stem.* It can sometimes be done, but it is never quite a complete and satisfactory job. The old false proverb, "It is never too late to be what you might have been," should be changed to, "It is always too late to be what you might have been."

Besides this difficulty there is the permanent loss of those who resist or escape all efforts at reclamation and never develop religious interests or establish connections with the church. More than half of the adults in this country to-day are without church relations or any practical interest in religion.

Now, it may be admitted at the start that no program of religious education that could be devised would

49

wholly remedy this unhappy situation. No system planned and carried out by human agencies can be altogether efficient. Yet it is a much simpler and more practicable thing to keep children from going spiritually astray than to win them back once the spiritual bonds are broken and the habits of the life set in another direction. A little prevention is more effective than much cure in this realm. Who can believe that if the church would devote itself fully and effectively to the religious nurture and training of childhood the next generation would see more than half of these individuals indifferent to the claims of religion and cold or hostile to the church!

THE TESTIMONY OF THE CHURCH ITSELF

What is the testimony of the church itself as to the effectiveness of education as a method of inculcating religion? Or has the church made a sufficient trial of the educational method to be able to judge of its results? Most of the Protestant Church has not.

It may be objected that the church does believe in religious education, else why the Sunday school, which is connected with almost every church no matter how small? True, the church has the Sunday school, and in a moderate sort of way believes in it. Yet, as has already been said, the church has used the Sunday school chiefly as an evangelistic and not as an educational agency. Nor does it believe in the Sunday school enough to cause it to make the Sunday school much more than an appendage, a minor supplement or adjunct to what are conceived to be the church's main activities, namely, preaching, worship, and evangelism for adult congregations.

Another proof that the church has not believed deeply

in religious education as a fundamental means of cultivating religion is the fact that it has not questioned until recently, and most of the church does not yet question, whether the amount of instruction which can be given in Sunday school is adequate to meet the needs of the child. The right of religion to a part of the week-day time or to some time in the vacation period is a new thought which the Protestant Church is just now taking up.

There emerges in connection with this point, however, a most convincing and inspiring evidence of the value of the educational method in religion. This is that while the Sunday school is, as a rule, made incidental to the remainder of the church program, its teachers largely untrained, its equipment usually poor, its organization and administration often inefficient, its method anything but educational in the true sense of the word, even with all this handicap the Sunday school is undoubtedly the most fruitful of the church's present-day enterprises in the actual making of Christians and the grounding of moral characters. Indeed, the church owes a very large proportion of its membership to this neglected part of its organization. What might not the church accomplish through such an educational agency if it would take it seriously and make the religious training of children its first concern!

The Roman Catholic among all the churches has been the most consistent in the use of the educational method in religion. So insistent is this church that religion shall be made an integral part of the education of its young that Catholic children are withdrawn in large numbers from the public schools and sent to the schools of the church, where they are taught religion along with their geography and grammar.

This statement is not meant to approve the particular type of methods used by the Catholic Church; the pedagogy it employs is generations behind the best method of the day and grievously ineffective. Nor is the statement meant to approve the materials taught; many of them are utterly unadapted both to the learner and to the aims sought. It certainly is not meant to approve the withdrawal of children from the public schools in order to educate them in parochial schools; this is a handicap to the children and, if the policy should become universal among the churches, would be a blow to progress and a danger to the republic.

What is meant to be pointed out is that the Catholic Church, in spite of its inefficiency in the use of the educational method, nevertheless makes that method work. For who believes that, did the Catholic Church depend on the method of adult evangelism to win adherents to its faith and membership, it could attract any large number to a theology so out of accord with the spirit of modern times, to a church autocracy whose head resides in a distant country and whose policy runs counter to the genius of democracy, or to a religious organization so out of harmony with American ideals and the temper of the times! Let the Catholic Church in the United States educate its young in religious matters as carelessly as the average Protestant church and it would break down in a generation. The leaders of the Catholic Church know this, hence their zeal for religious education. Would that all Protestant churches were as wise in the matter of policy! Let the Protestant churches of this country adopt the policy of the Catholic Church as to the *stress to be placed on religious education* in the promotion of religion, using at the same time the better educational method available to

52

the churches, and there is no reasonable objective that could not be reached in the field of religious achievement.

Religion can be attained by the processes of gradual growth and unfoldment in the life of an individual. This is abundantly proved in the experience of many persons of the finest spiritual qualities. The developing life can be saved by careful nurture and training, that is, by proper education in religion, from drifting into spiritual coldness, indifference or rebellion. This process of religious development, while it does not deny the possibility of reclamatory conversion, is the safer, more natural and fruitful, and the one which should above all others first be sought by those agencies which have responsibility for the religious welfare of the children and youth—the home, the church school, the church.

CHAPTER V

RELIGION THROUGH EVANGELISM

CERTAIN fundamental distinctions between the educational and the evangelistic program in religion have already been discussed (Chapter II). While they differ widely in their methods, the most fundamental difference between these two programs is in the *presuppositions* from which they start and in the immediate *ends* sought.

The educational method presupposes a child at the start nonmoral and nonreligious, capable of being made by environment and education either immoral or moral, either irreligious or religious. The evangelistic method presupposes that whatever may be the child's original status, it is necessary ultimately for him to pass through a process of conversion, before he can enter fully into the kingdom.

Naturally the radically different presuppositions lead to the seeking of different ends as the immediate goals of effort. The educational method aims primarily at *conserving*, the evangelistic method at *reclaiming*. The procedure by which each of these ends is to be attained determines the program to be followed under each system.

HOW THE CHURCH CAME BY THE EVANGELISTIC METHOD

From one point of view it is incomprehensible how so large a proportion of the Protestant Church came to stress evangelistic work for adults ahead of educational work for children. From another point of view the reason for this placing of emphasis is entirely clear.

RELIGION THROUGH EVANGELISM

The Protestant Church came into existence as a protest against spiritual deadness, moral corruption, and the decay of religion. Formalism, pretense, and chicanery ruled and had long ruled in the church. Personal religious experience, direct responsibility of an individual to God, and ethical dynamic coming from a living faith were practically unknown. The body of Christianity was still alive but its soul was dead.

Naturally, the leaders of the new church saw the necessity of changing this situation if Christianity was to be saved. Men must be called to repentance and led to seek regeneration of corrupt lives. The power of the Spirit to bring back to life the spiritually dead must be proved. The transforming power of a vital faith must be put to the test. Men and women must be converted, hence religious revivals were needed. The Wesleys, Whitefield, and other great evangelists later took the field and did a marvelous work. New life came back into the church, religion again became a living spirit and power, righteous living once more became the true expression of Christianity.

For the Protestant Church of that day the problem was, first of all, a problem of reaching the adults and introducing them to a living religion. In their spiritual deadness they had to be compelled, persuaded, driven into the kingdom of a new experience. The evangelistic method was probably the best way, possibly the only way of accomplishing that result.

Nor is the attitude of the church of that day with reference to the method to use with the children hard to understand once we grant the theology that then ruled with reference to the child's status. For if the child is out of harmony with God by the very fact of his existence until by a supreme and cyclonic spiritual upheaval he struggles free from the trammels of an evil nature inherited from Adam; and if, once this cyclonic experience of conversion has been accomplished the child is sufficiently "saved," then manifestly *reclamation* is the great need and the entire program of the church must be planned to that end.

The doctrine of hereditary guilt, based on the assumption that Adam was literally the head of the human race, that his acts were the acts of the race, and that in his sin all posterity sinned, was first brought into Christian theology in the fifth century by Augustine. He says, "The infant who is lost is punished because he belongs to the mass of perdition and as a child of Adam is justly condemned." Calvin adopted and developed these views, and in the Reformation they passed over into English theology. Calvin taught concerning the status of children: "They bring condemnation with them from their mother's womb—They are odious and abominable to God." This view was incorporated in the Westminster Confession and in practically all the other Confessions of the period of reconstruction.

Wesley took the position that children are "members of the kingdom" and that such "membership assumes regeneration." Following the lead of its founder, the Methodist Church has continuously committed itself to this view of the child's status, the latest statement being a reiteration of the position by the General Conference of 1920.

Other religious bodies, under the influence of a more humane outlook upon life, the acceptance of the doctrine of evolution, and a clearer sense of the Fatherhood of God, have softened their stern theologies on this point to the extent that the old doctrine of "original sin" and "natural depravity" has lost much of its sway.

Its effects are yet being felt, however, in the *program* of the church, whatever may be its theology. Even in the Methodist Church, one of the most clearly outspoken of all on the question of the child being at the beginning right with God, the central program of activities *has subordinated the conservation of the child to the reclamation of adults*.

No doubt one important reason for the relatively great emphasis placed on adult evangelism is that this is in a sense the most obvious and the easiest method. The results by this method are more immediate and striking. The educational process works slowly. Character, morality, and the realization of spiritual ideals come but gradually, and without special emotional exhilaration or excitement. It is in human nature to respond to the striking, the cataclysmic, the sudden. A cloudburst excites wonder and awe, but the gradual drawing of the water which fell in the storm up from the earth by the steady, quiet power of the sun goes on without attracting our notice. A thousand converts "hitting the sawdust trail" will cause much more thrill and comment than ten thousand children advancing quietly line upon line and precept upon precept toward enlightened Christian character and attainment.

Furthermore, evangelistic campaigns come cheaper financially than educational programs. It costs less to finance an evangelistic campaign lasting a few weeks, even with a modern high-salaried evangelist, than an educational program running for a dozen years. It costs less not only in money, but in thought, in planning, in effort, in study, and in day-by-day oversight and guidance. The evangelistic way is therefore the easy way, the cheap way. If it would work as efficiently as the educational way, it would be the best way just because it is the simpler, the easier, and the cheaper. The difficulty is that it does not work as a substitute for the longer drawn out, slower, less sensational but altogether more effective educational process in religion.

THE EVANGELISTIC METHOD HAS AN IMPORTANT PLACE

There is, nevertheless, a very definite place for evangelism and the evangelistic method in the program of the church. Great numbers of men and women need to be converted—are being converted under the evangelistic program of the church. None who have been fair and impartial observers of the work of reaching indifferent or irreligious persons through the agencies commonly employed in evangelistic effort have failed to be convinced that human lives are often regenerated and transformed by something that happens to them in connection with conversion and its consequences. The fruits of this regeneration and transformation are seen in changed morals, new objectives, and in inner sense of harmony with a divine power and plan. The church should carry on a large program of this spiritual reclamation.

Yet it must be conceded that every reclamatory conversion is evidence of a failure and a spiritual tragedy. Dante says a tragedy is "a bad ending of a good beginning." Each of these spiritually reclaimed ones over whose conversion we rejoice had a good beginning; he was at one time right with God, standing at the entrance of two paths, one of which leads to an increasingly broadening and deepening sense of relationship with God, the other of which leads away from the consciousness of religious values and to the necessity of a special act of divine power and grace to bring the individual back to a recognition of spiritual things. Let us repeat, there is no greater tragedy than the need to reclaim a soul that should not have been allowed to go astray.

Evangelism is therefore essentially a method for adults—for those who, either from lack of religious nurture and training in childhood or from some combination of circumstances have failed to respond to religious influences and have grown up to years of conscious self-direction ignorant of these things, indifferent to them, or in a state of spiritual disaffection. Evangelism should be a supplement to the method of religious education. It should seek, on the one hand, to reclaim those who, because of failure in the religious educational system or because of failure of the child to respond to it, drift away from the church and spiritual interests. It should seek, on the other hand, to reclaim all possible of those who have had no opportunity at religious education and so are naturally indifferent and ignorant in religious matters. The real work of evangelism should be to "mop up" after religious education, gathering in all possible of those whom it has missed.

But in no case should the church neglect its educational program for its evangelistic. Conservation of childhood should never give way to reclamation of adults. A child kept in the "way" is better than a grown person returned to that "way." Furthermore, the more effective the program of religious education is made the less will be the need for reclamation.

RESULTS OF THE EVANGELISTIC PROGRAM

Certain undesirable results are bound to follow from the evangelistic system, especially if it is not combined with a definite system of religious education. One of these is an unintelligent, untrained church constituency, ignorant of the Bible and of the great fundamentals of religious thought and faith. Another is the inevitable and perfectly natural tendency of the untrained convert to "fall from grace," to "backslide," and to require to be reconverted.

One who has lived a life of spiritual neutrality or hostility may be challenged, convicted of sin, brought to repentance and conversion. This has occurred tens of thousands of times. A new set of motives, new goals of ambition, new ideals of conduct are set up. The things that were loved are now hated and the things that were hated are now loved. The new convert joins the church, receives the joyful welcome of preacher and congregation, and is now one of the elect in a very real and true sense. And yet . . . The man who was before ignorant of the Bible is ignorant of it still; he who was unfamiliar with the simple but potent message of Jesus is ignorant of it still. He who has lacked a knowledge of the great characters of the Bible and of the church is ignorant still. He who was a religious illiterate is illiterate still.

Conversion may reconstruct the motive forces of life and reorganize its powers, but it does not supply the fundamental knowledge, intelligence, and information upon which alone true Christianity can be built.

So the church that has any vision or sense of obligation is inevitably committed to the education of its constituency even if it depends primarily on the method of evangelistic reclamation for its members. If it does not educate children and youth in religious matters, it will in the end be obliged to educate these same persons after, older grown, they are reclaimed by conversion.

And they educate more easily and naturally by far if it is done in the earlier years.

As a matter of fact, however, the church usually does not educate its converts any more than it does its children; perhaps not so much. Seeming to assume that the great thing needful is accomplished when the new convert is able to testify to a conscious acceptance by the Divine, the church is all too prone to open the doors of membership, enter the new name on the church roll, and call the whole matter closed. The result is an unintelligent, confused Christian whose emotional exaltation soon passes away and who, lacking the great basic religious concepts that can develop only by the slow process of teaching and learning, either becomes discouraged, thinks he was mistaken or deceived, and drops the whole matter.

What a tragically large proportion of those who have embraced the Christian life under the influence of an evangelistic appeal soon fall away into a state of indifference! In such cases the seed falls on ready soil and springs up quickly, but the soil is not rich and deep through thorough cultivation, hence the new growth quickly dies down. Conversion is usually accomplished under high emotional tension. It is followed by a feeling of deep peace, satisfaction, and soul quiet or exaltation. The change from the previous unrest and unhappiness is so marked that the entire world seems changed. Life can never be the same humdrum thing again. The way ahead glows with a beautifully radiant light. And thus the new convert enters hopefully, confidently on the way.

But emotional heights (or depths) do not last. It is not in human nature to live constantly on the highest altitudes nor in the deepest valleys. Tension tends to relax. Feeling becomes less keen. The contrast between the old state and the new grows less striking. Something of the radiance expressing a glow of inner feeling dims out. Things are settling back into their old perspective. Life has something of routine and humdrum and commonplace just as it had before. Questions begin to arise! Was I mistaken, did I only think I was converted? Am I of such a nature that I cannot "hold out"? Am I drifting back? *Am* I a Christian after all?

Some such cruel and soul-numbing experience has been passed through by numberless persons who might, by preparatory training, have been saved from the sweating of blood which the disillusioning process entails.

Those who have been properly instructed in what it means to be a Christian; who have been led to give proper balance to religious thought, feeling, and action from early childhood, and who are not led to stake their entire religious certitude on the play of a fluctuating emotion will escape such an experience when the time comes for them to make a personal acceptance of the Christian way they have been taught. Nor, having once made this personal decision, will there be the danger of shipwreck on the ground of a changing mood. For the person who has a well-grounded set of religious concepts that have grown up with him from childhood, who has a well-defined set of religious habits expressing themselves normally in such acts as prayer, worship, and service, who is religiously *intelligent*, is secure against the accidents of temporary emotional changes.

CHAPTER VI

THE CHURCH'S NEGLECT OF RELIGIOUS EDUCATION

THE Protestant Church has never taken religious education seriously. This seems a strange, an ungracious, even a false thing to say of a church that has founded schools and colleges by the hundred, that, indeed, preceded the state in its support of general education. Nevertheless, it is true—the church has never taken *religious* education seriously. It has been a great believer in and promoter of general education but not of religious education. The proofs of this proposition form the content of the present chapter.

HOW THE SUNDAY SCHOOL CAME TO THE CHURCH

It is strikingly true in the history of human institutions that progressive movements and reforms often come from other sources than those where we should naturally turn for leadership. This has been true for the church, some of whose most important movements have originated entirely outside the professional and official group commissioned by the church to guide its destinies.

Robert Raikes is credited with the initiation of the Sunday school. Robert Raikes was an English manufacturer and merchant. He possessed no great learning; certainly, he was no theologian. A member of the Church of England in a time when the state had not yet taken responsibility for general education, Raikes was impressed with the ignorance, the vice, and the squalor of the children of the poor in Gloucester, England. They were illiterate, profane, dirty, ragged, ill-mannered, immoral.

Free schools did not exist, and their parents were unable to pay tuition for their education, even had they been interested enough in education to do so. Social outcasts, neglected by state and church, ignored by society, they were a reproach to the civilization of their day. Robert Raikes said they must be taught—taught religion and the rudiments of education. So he hired teachers, and paid them a shilling or so a day from his own pocket. He secured the use of a part of the church for his classes, which met on Sunday for several hours. The children were taught personal cleanliness, good manners, reading, writing, numbers—and religion; a curriculum suspiciously like the general education program with religion added.

At first many of the churches were opposed to this profanation of the Lord's Day and of the church with the teaching of the children. The Archbishop of Canterbury thundered against this new movement. Many of the churches closed their doors to it. But the movement had life, so it grew in spite of opposition; first despised, then tolerated, at last adopted by the church which had not the vision to inaugurate the movement itself. As provision was made for the free general education of children in England the secular subjects were dropped from the Sunday school curriculum and its aims centered on religion; though to this day the Sunday school movement in the Church of England has never been quite popular among the social classes. The stigma of its lowly origin still clings to it.

When, a century and a quarter ago, American Protestantism took up the Sunday-school idea there was far from unanimity upon it. At first many of the churches opposed it. Some closed their doors to the Sunday classes, urging that it was unfit that God's house should be put to such uses. The church was a place for worship, for prayer, for preaching, and none should profane the the sacred edifice by bringing into it the teaching of children. Here, again, however, the forces for education finally won and the Sunday school about one hundred years ago became a recognized part of the church's legitimate enterprises.

RELIGIOUS EDUCATION LOOKED UPON AS INCIDENTAL

During no period of its history, however, has the Sunday school been looked upon by those in control of the church as a major enterprise. In making up the program of the church as a whole, or the program of an individual unit, religious education of children has been planned for and provided for only after other interests had been taken care of.

There have been many worthy projects planned and carried out by the church. There have been great missionary campaigns which brought splendidly to the consciousness and the conscience of the church the needs of the less fortunate in this and other lands. There have been great campaigns for group and personal evangelism which have netted many souls reclaimed. There have been educational campaigns, seeking moral and monetary support for church colleges and other secular schools of the church. There have been great financial campaigns netting scores of millions of dollars for the church to expend on its excellent enterprises. Now, all of these are worthy projects and most of them were well carried out. There is no disposition on our part to criticize or do anything but admire and approve this splendid work. But the question still remains, *just when did the church have a great campaign for the promotion of the cause of religious education?*

Consider the program of Sunday services of the church. It is built primarily around the interests of adults. In many churches the choicest hour of the forenoon, the time most convenient for adults after late rising, a leisurely breakfast and preparation for church, is taken for the "regular service"; the Sunday school coming at the close of the forenoon, at a time when children on other days usually have dinner or lunch and when the day has lost for them its best of spirits and freshness. True, in some churches the children are recently being given a more favorable hour, but the more general practice is yet to consult the convenience and wishes of the adults first, the children being secondary.

The advice is quite generally given to parents by church leaders that children should be taken to the church preaching service in preference to any other exercise of the church. When the children come to this service they find almost nothing they can understand, little they can intelligently feel, and practically nothing they can do except to sit in an agony of suppressed wriggling longing for the ending to come. It is a service *of* adults, *for* adults and *by* adults. Yet by strange confusion of thought there are those who believe this the best way to train the child in religion! Paul was a preacher rather than an educator, but he had some well-defined notions about the futility of forcing strong meat upon babes.

That the church has had little interest in the educational method in religion is seen in the course prescribed for the training of its ministers. They are, of course, trained primarily as theologians and preachers. They must have courses in historical theology, in systematic theology, and in practical theology. They must know Greek and Hebrew in order to skill in biblical exegesis.

They must study the principles and art of sermon structure in order to convince, persuade, move—adults. They must master the arts of speech in order to smooth and effective public utterance. They must train themselves in the methods of evangelism in order successfully to conduct campaigns for converts.

Here, again, we have a list of things all of which are good. But where does the training of the minister for religious education come in? I am aware that most theological seminaries now offer a few courses in religious education. Some of them even require some four hours out of about ninety demanded for the degree. Not a few offer no religious education work of any kind nor take any note of its importance.

So it happens that most ministers go out from their three years of seminary work with little or no training for the hardest task they will confront, for the hardest task the church confronts. It is easy enough for them to preach well-organized sermons out of a well-stocked mind to a congregation of well-ordered adults. But in the presence of the *children*, with their infinitely greater needs and their infinitely more difficult demands, the preacher is relatively helpless. *Nor is it primarily his fault.* In a day of education and of educational experts, a day when the church should change its method and its stress from a program primarily of preaching to adults to a program which provides first of all for the *teaching of children* in religion, the church trains its leaders and workers in everything except the most important and difficult thing they have to do.

No wonder, therefore, that the average preacher feels somewhat helpless before a group of children. No wonder he watches with a sigh of relief his "junior congregation" file out after the ten-minute sermon that was much harder to prepare than the thirty-minute sermon that will follow. No wonder that the preacher not infrequently leaves the Sunday school largely to the superintendent and officers, concerning himself with it only to see that it turns in fairly satisfactory reports as to attendance and collections.

And no wonder either that hundreds of young ministers, awakening to the fact that the chief problem of their church concerns itself with education, are crying out against a system that leaves them unprepared for the greatest opportunity and responsibility that rests upon the church. The church should make training in religious education one of the chief lines in the preparation of its ministers.

Possibly the most immediately obvious evidence of the church's failure to realize the importance of religious education is seen in the architecture of its church buildings. It is evident, of course, that the church structure has been built for adults. The central aspect is an audience room, a place for grown-ups to listen to preaching. When the adults have been taken care of, there may be some Sunday school rooms provided—as a supplement or an afterthought to the main plan of the building. But even these are usually highly insufficient in number and capacity, and inadequate for their purpose.

If the church ever becomes a true *teaching* institution, centering its best efforts on serving its children instead of selfishly looking out for its adults; if those of us who are in charge shall refuse to take the best seats in the synagogue for ourselves regardless of the helpless little ones; if we really go at it to set a child in our midst as the goal of our church effort, then the church architects and building committees will need to study their problems anew. When this day comes, as please God it will come before a great while, these architects and builders can learn much by going to the public schools and studying their architecture. Here the purpose is first of all to provide for *teaching*, though the assembly (audience) room is not omitted from the scheme. The result is a highly effective working plant for the development of the whole life of the pupil.

The relative importance assigned religious education of children in the estimation of the church may be discovered from the distribution of funds in its budget. The things that people believe in and care for they are willing to pay for; the things they esteem of little value or think about but little they do not consider spending money for. Willingness to supply economic support is then one practical test of the interest and esteem in which the membership of the church holds its various enterprises.

Now, it is a well-known fact that in general the Sunday school is supported by the pennies of the children who attend. True, many churches are coming to add a small amount annually to their budget for the support of the Sunday school, but this is the exception rather than the rule. Not only is this true, but the Sunday schools of one denomination at least are expected to pay an aggregate of two hundred thousand dollars a year toward the support of the board which manages the Sunday school activities of the denomination. Sunday schools are poorly equipped in reference to books, teaching supplies, professional libraries for teachers, etc., because the church "cannot afford it."

It all comes down finally to what the church believes in or wants to spend its money for. A certain church recently had a local budget of over thirty thousand dollars, one thousand of which was assigned to religious education. In this church there was a pastor's assistant on a salary of three thousand; an office secretary on a salary of twelve hundred; paid singers on salaries of four thousand; the support of a city mission on an expenditure of about five thousand. The minister had a salary of about six thousand. The matter of a director of religious education came up, but the church "could not afford it." The question of week day religious education for children was discussed, but the church "had no more funds for religious education." In this church budget the adults were willing to spend approximately thirty dollars on themselves to one dollar spent on the children of the church for religion. They were willing to hire professional singers to sing to the adult congregation for fifteen or twenty minutes each Sunday, paying them ninety dollars for the service rendered, but could not find money to equip properly for teaching their children nor for paying for week-day teachers or directors for their classes in religion. While these figures and the details will vary from church to church, the example cited is so nearly typical that it may, with generous and increasing exceptions, be called characteristic of the church.

Another indication of the center of emphasis in the church is found in the trend which conspicuous greatness among its leaders has taken. Greatness commonly takes the direction of the most pressing social demand and the willingness of institutions to pay in honors, position, or money for service rendered.

The church has had great evangelists, great missionaries, great theologians, great scholars, great artists, great preachers, great reformers, all willing to give of their talent or their genius to the church and making thereby a great contribution. But where are the great educators in the service of the church? They have been few. This has not been because great educators have not been interested in religion and childhood and the church, but because the church has not invited them, welcomed their services, or made a place for them. Hence it is that now, when the church is beginning to realize the importance of education in religion, she has few trained educators in her service and must perforce suffer the blind to lead the blind or else call upon the ranks of secular education to supply the skilled leadership her own program has failed to develop.

RELIGIOUS EDUCATION IN CHURCH COLLEGES

Let no one ascribe the church's lack of interest in religious education to a lack of interest in *education*. The church has for centuries, as we have said, made the promotion of education one of its chief concerns, and its schools constitute one of the brightest pages in its history. The earliest colleges founded in this country were founded by the church. Far more than half of all the higher institutions in the United States to-day were church founded and many of them still are, in part at least, church supported. The church-founded colleges and universities accommodate approximately half of those who receive higher education in this country.

Yet, strange to say, religion occupies so small a place as to be almost negligible in the curriculum of the church colleges. In almost none of them is instruction in religion on as secure a financial and academic basis as mathematics, science, philosophy, or like subjects. The college asks for the support of church people on the ground of the religious influence of the school, but seems to assume that religion can be appropriated from the general atmosphere and environment and need not be especially provided for as a study for the classrooms. Indeed, on this score there is comparatively little choice between the church college and the state institution. Here again, then, it is evident that the church does not believe strongly in religious education, for its own particular schools set apart to "train leaders" teach almost everything excepting religion.

CHAPTER VII

IF THE CHURCH SHOULD ADOPT AN EDUCATIONAL PROGRAM

THE writer recently came before his class of seventy-seven young ministers with the following proposition which he asked them to consider in all its bearings and determine whether or not it is true: *The primary responsibility and obligation of the church, standing above all other responsibilities and obligations whatsoever, is the religious education of its childhood and youth.* After full and deliberate thought all but four answered in the affirmative, thus committing the church so far as they are concerned to the religious education of the young as its primary function.

Manifestly, the unanimity of position taken required that another question be asked these men. It was put to them in this form: *If the foregoing proposition is true, what are its implications: what should the church do about it?*

This is probably the most important question confronting the Christian church to-day. Here is a church which in an era favorable for its development and expression has barely been holding its own; no, let us be frank; it has been losing ground. Now, it is offered an instrument, proved in other fields than the church, which can readily be adapted to the uses of the church and through which it is reasonably certain that the church can recover lost ground and enter upon new territory. This instrument is religious education. What will the church do about it?

In order to make religious education its primary enterprise in practice, great and fundamental changes will have to be made by the church. These changes cannot be made in a day. Many of them cannot be completely made in a decade. But, under wise leadership, all the changes can be put under way and developed as rapidly as conditions will permit.

AN EDUCATIONAL LEADERSHIP

Fundamental to an educational program for the church is a true *educational* leadership. No enterprise can succeed if managed by those who are not fully in sympathy with it, or those who do not understand its fundamental aims, or those not equipped with the skill of technique necessary to the operation of the enterprise.

Freely granting certain notable exceptions, it may fairly be asserted that the present leadership of the church is not an educational leadership. This is said without thought or intention of criticism of present leaders, many of whom have rendered service beyond praise to the church. But most of these men have come up through another regime. To them the great work of the church has been to "preach the gospel." The pulpit has been their throne, the preacher the man called of God to the most important work given man to do as a colaborer with the Divine, the proclaiming of glad tidings to lost souls.

To such men, themselves usually great and inspiring preachers and men grown gray in the service of this great ideal, it is natural and perhaps inevitable that other phases of the church's program should be secondary to preaching. They may believe in a way in the work of the Sunday school, believe even in the expansion of the program of Sunday instruction to the work of week-day classes in religion, or to vacation church day schools; but as to making the educational enterprise of the church its chief concern, the *first* thing planned for in its policies, the pearl of great price which the church should sell all else to buy. . . .

It is humanly impossible for most men well past middle life, as the leaders of the church naturally are, to make so complete a reversal of brain paths as this position would require. They may see the validity of the new program, they may wish it well, they may even mean to give it their support; but most of them will nevertheless, unintentionally or not, have a background of reservations, a set of conflicting ideals and habits of mind, speech and action, which will qualify or negate their support of the new project.

The control of the church should gradually, but without unnecessary delay, be taken over by those possessed of the educational ideal for the church. Usually, though with notable exceptions, this will mean by the younger men who, in connection with their training for service in the church have given a prominent place to the study of religious education and who understand both its possibilities and its limitations. Such men will, of course, know religious educational method. They will understand its problems and principles of organization and administration. They will know how so to plan the program of the church that the religious nurture and training of children shall become its primary concern, without at the same time neglecting the other enterprises of the church.

It goes without saying that these religious educational leaders will have to be developed and trained. The church has now relatively few men who by training, conviction, and experience are able to assume leadership such as that required in this new field. But the number qualified to do this is increasing. Prospective ministers in the theological schools are not only gladly taking the required courses in religious education, but many of them are electing as freely as their requirements will permit the courses in religious education and general education from adjoining university departments. These men are in earnest; they see the great opportunity before them to serve the church and the cause of religion, and the next decade will witness numbers of them beginning to forge ahead into positions of educational leadership now unoccupied because none are ready to fill them. The success of the church in the years that lie ahead will depend in no small degree on the wisdom and capacity for leadership manifested by its *ministers of education*.

A NEW EMPHASIS IN THE TRAINING OF ITS MINISTRY

If the point of view set forth in the preceding section is accepted, we are immediately led to a second inevitable conclusion: The church must change the emphasis in the training of its ministry. The tradition is deeply grounded that the minister shall be trained as a theologian and a preacher. One young minister-in-training, puzzled by conflicting claims for preeminence between the evangelistic and the educational ideal for the church, exclaimed, "But surely our *great* commission as servants of the church is to preach the gospel, is it not?"

"Not if I understand the matter," answered his instructor. "I understand your great commission to be that of bringing the world to *know and follow the teachings and example of Jesus.* If you can do this best by preaching, that is your great commission. If you can do it best by teaching, then that is your great commission."

Preaching, like teaching, is a means and not an end.

It will not serve for the schools supplied by the church for the training of its ministers to admit half grudgingly a few courses on religious education as a concession to the demands of the times, allowing these to supplement a broad and dominating requirement in theology, the languages, and exegesis. The door must be thrown wide open and without any grudging. If the educational method can be made and should be made the chief instrument of the church in gathering, training, and holding its constituency, then there is no place for half-way measures. The church must acknowledge this method and prepare its ministers to handle it successfully. Training in the principles and methods of religious education must not be incidental and perfunctory, something *added on* to the real and fundamental preparation for their work, an important accessory, but still an accessory.

These men must come from their preparation not only with some knowledge of religious educational method, but with the educational ideal prominent in their minds, the educational viewpoint dominant in their thought and plans. Anything less than this will not serve if the church sets out really to take religious education seriously as a highly important function.

One of the first requisites of the minister is to be grounded through his training in the educational viewpoint for religion, is to supply him with an *educational atmosphere* in which to get his training. It is doubtful whether this can be done in the average theological seminary of the present day. This is not meant as a criticism on the seminaries, but the fact, of course, is that the traditions and atmosphere of the theological schools do not favor the educational method. They have for generations been of another kind, and such things cannot be changed offhand and at will.

Doubtless some of the schools of theology will make an honest effort to meet the new conditions. There are indications that some are already attempting to do so. Those seminaries that are connected with universities will effect the transformation with least difficulty, for the university departments of general education and religious education are at hand to supply the educational tone and train to the educational ideal.

However the details may be worked out, it seems inevitable that the courses offered by the church for the training of the ministers must be still further liberalized in the direction of practical training for the demands which the church program of the future must of necessity put upon its minister. The great problems of the average minister are no longer, as they once were, problems of theology, of exegesis, of refined and hair-splitting exposition of controversial problems. Most Christian churches of to-day are thoroughly agreed upon enough great fundamentals to save the world if only these fundamentals could be made effective in the lives of the people. The great problem of the church in this age is to make of itself the effective instrument by which the basic Christian truths can be planted in the minds and hearts of youth and so cultivated, nurtured, and guarded that they shall come to fruitage as Christian character in adults.

IF THE CHURCH SHOULD ADOPT A PROGRAM

For many years the smaller churches will have to be content with one minister to carry out all functions of the church. The man who preaches the sermons and acts as pastor will in addition have to be business manager, director of religious education, director of recreation, and responsible for whatever additional program the church assumes. This wide diversity of responsibility precludes highly specialized training in any particular line, thus making the office of the minister in this type of church correspond somewhat to that of general family practitioner in the field of medicine.

In larger and stronger churches, however, the time is undoubtedly coming when there will be a specialized ministry covering various lines of activity within the local church. Second to none in this group of ministers should be the minister of education. His position should be coordinate with that of the minister of preaching. His general and professional preparation for the work should be commensurate with the responsibilities involved, which are certainly not less than those of the pulpit. The financial compensation should not suffer in comparison with that for the preaching minister.

The minister of education should, under the educational committee of the church, have responsibility for the planning and administration of the educational program in all of its branches and divisions. He should recommend or appoint teachers, assign them to classes, be responsible for the grading and promotion of pupils, determine curriculum requirements, and carry out all other such administrative functions under the general oversight of the committee.

A number of denominations have already provided for this office, recognizing officially the minister of education though not always as coordinate in power and responsibility with the preaching minister, who is held primarily responsible for all interests and activities of the church.

Not until the educational ministry of the church is recognized and provided for, first in the preparation of the general preaching ministry, and, second, in the training and employment of a highly specialized educational ministry when the size of the church permits, will the interests of religious education be fully recognized in the economy of the church.

CHANGE OF EMPHASIS IN CHURCH PROGRAM

If the church is to make religious education its great concern there must be a distinct change in emphasis at certain points of its program. At the present time, as we have seen, religious education does not receive great relative emphasis at the hands of the church. Some of the tests of the importance placed on any enterprise by the church are the following:

1. The amount of time, thought, energy expended compared with the magnitude of the problem or the work to be done.

2. The amount of money expended compared with the need for funds in order to secure efficiency.

3. The place occupied by the enterprise in the interest and esteem of the church as compared with its other enterprises.

4. The place given the interests and problems of the enterprise in the councils, discussions, and plans of church leaders.

5. The relative efficiency and success in carrying out the enterprise as compared with the efficiency and success in other enterprises.

Measured by such tests as these, it is probable that the major enterprises of the church as conceived by its present leaders would be listed somewhat in this order:

1. Preaching; ministry for adult congregations.
2. Evangelism; efforts to secure reclamatory conversions.
3. Missionary activities; at home and abroad.
4. General education; schools and colleges.
5. Religious education; chiefly in Sunday schools.
6. Publishing; religious books, papers, etc.

This is to say, measured by the tests suggested, religious education probably does not come higher than fifth from the head of a list of six of the church's leading activities of the present. At least it certainly is a long way from coming *first*.

Let it again be reiterated in this connection that in making such a comparison there is no thought of disparaging any of the other great and worthy enterprises of the church. The point is that religious education should come first because *it is at the root of all the others*. Religious education will create an intelligent and loyal congregation for the preacher; even where reclamatory evangelism proves necessary it will in some degree have prepared the soil for the reception of the message of the evangelist and for the action of divine grace in the heart; it will broaden the sympathies and increase the intelligence of our people with reference to missionary needs; it will supply the motives which will insure the proper use of the powers developed through general education; it will train and educate a reading public for religious materials published by the church. The purpose of religious education is, therefore, not to supplant or overtop other activities of the church, but only to lay firm and strong the foundations on which they all may build. This it can do and will do if given a chance.

If this is to be accomplished, the church must get a new perspective on the relative importance of its enterprises. It must not undertake to build without foundations. It must see to it that religious education is given the full measure which its importance demands of the time, thought, and energy of the church; that it has its proper share of the church's funds; that in public interest and esteem it takes high rank; that in actual working efficiency and achieved results it does not suffer when compared with other church enterprises. In order to accomplish these results great and fundamental changes of emphasis must be made in the program of the church.

A REDISTRIBUTION OF THE CHURCH'S BUDGET

The church, as an organization, spends comparatively little on the religious education of its young. Now, conceivably this might come either from the possibility of getting the necessary teaching done free, as in the home and in the Sunday school, or it might come from failure to recognize that here is one of the most fruitful places for the expenditure of church funds.

So little does the average church look upon the religious education of children as a thing to be paid for that it usually does not even put an appropriation for the Sunday school in its budget, or, as we have already seen, if it does, the amount is so small that it is practically negligible. The members of the Sunday school by their own contributions pay for their lesson materials or other supplies required.

Now, this is not meant to argue that the pupils in the Sunday school should not pay toward the support of the church and its enterprises; they should, for this is a part not only of their obligation, but of their training. They should, however, pay toward the support of their *church*, and then in addition, class by class or the school as a whole, should directly contribute to various benevolent, religious, and missionary enterprises as opportunity offers.

The point is that the religious education of its children, in the Sunday school or whatever other schools of religion the church may run, is a vital part of the church's program and should come in on the distribution of its budget the same as the expenditure for preaching, benevolences, missionary work, and the like. The financing of this important function of the church should not be something supplemental, a side line, an extra to be taken care of by odds and ends of subscription, or a gift now and then to make up for a deficit. In fact, one of the best tests of the church's regard for religious education is the way it is treated in the church budget.

Besides the change of policy here suggested the church must, if it is to make religious education a primary interest, spend much more money on this work than has been done in the past. The teaching in the Sunday school should probably for the most part continue at least for the present to be done without pay. The supervision should, at least in all larger schools, be paid for, and the amount of preparation and time devoted to it correspondingly increased. In the largest schools the supervisors of departments should receive a moderate compensation and then make a real profession out of their work. To those who fear that such service would lose its fine quality if paid for, we need but say that this objection does not seem to hold for the preacher

(who at first was not paid for his work) nor the missionary (who likewise formerly worked without pay).

When the church takes up week-day instruction in
religion and vacation church schools in a large way, as
it must do if it is to make religious education a leading
interest, then it must be prepared to spend thousands
where it is now spending hundreds of dollars. For these
systems cannot be run on a basis of free service. There
will be large bills to pay for teaching, for textbooks, and
for equipment.

APPLY EDUCATIONAL STANDARDS TO THE CHURCH SCHOOL

As has already been pointed out, the aims of the
church school in the past have hardly been educational
in the true sense. The child was expected to absorb
impressions from contact with the church and the
teacher. The mere "going to Sunday school" was supposed to possess some special spiritual potency able to
count for righteousness, no matter what went on there.
In all too many schools the standards of success and
efficiency have gone no further than:

Enrollment to-day 489; one year ago to-day 476
Attendance to-day 250; one year ago to-day 253
Teachers present   10; teachers absent   12
Visitors   5.
Collection $2.63; collection last Sunday $2.56.

Usually in the recording and presenting of such statistics as these there is no meaning, for there is no consideration of the relative success or failure of the system as reached by the figures shown. For example, if
the enrollment is 489, what *should* it be; how many
children rightfully within the sphere of influence of this
church are *not* enrolled; and who are they, and where

do they live, and why are they not here? If the attendance is 250 out of 489, what *should* it be; what is a fair average attendance based on enrollment; what is it for these same children in their public schools; why is it not larger here? If only 10 teachers out of 22 are present, where are the rest? Who are they? Is this a habit with the absentee group? Why are they not here to-day? If the collection is $2.63 for 250 people, is this about what it *should* be? If not, why is it not more?

But even when all these questions are answered in such a way as to make the statistics intelligible—as they seldom are—this is still only the *beginning;* for these things that the average school sets so much store by are but the preliminaries. The real question is, What are the *educational results* of our school? Thorndike tells us that education consists of "effecting desired changes in the lives of the pupils." What changes are the various classes effecting in the minds of their pupils? How efficient is the teaching? Is there any real study on the lessons? How much real spiritual development is going on? How much different in thought, life, ideals, character, loyalty to God and the church are the pupils for their contact with the Sunday school? It is evident, of course, that these questions do not admit of objective measurement and statistical statement in the same way that the other set of facts do. But they are not on that account the less important.

Nor are we wholly devoid of practical measure for these things. Suppose that each superintendent, each teacher, should take these three measures for the success of his work:

1. *What usable religious knowledge* are my pupils getting—about God, the Bible, the way of life set forth by Jesus?

2. *What religious attitudes* are they developing—interests, ideals, standards, loyalties toward the school, the church, the Bible, life itself?

3. *What practical applications* are they making of the truths taught and lessons learned to their daily living in the home, the school, the community, the world at large, etc.?

Would not a sober study of actual results on some such simple basis as this tend to disturb the complacency of many schools that now seem to be running so smoothly but which are measuring their success in terms of the simpler, more easily secured and more objective results?

Vitally related to this last problem, the real *educational* test of the church school, is the standard of the pupil's mastery of the curriculum, the extent to which he *knows*, *understands*, and *applies* the lessons he is taught. Religion involves a body of materials, chiefly but not wholly from the Bible, to be studied, remembered, repeated, discussed, applied, carried out into activity. Our standards on these points at present are lamentably low. Probably not one child in a hundred could pass such an examination on his Sunday-school material as he is required to pass month by month in his public-school studies in order to secure promotion. Yet the child must learn his religion and develop it in accordance with the same laws that govern his development in public school education.

The remedy at this point will necessitate better teaching. It will require better conditions under which teaching may go on, better classroom facilities, better equipment, more time available. It will also require somewhat radical revision of the curriculum which is offered the child.

A full discussion of the content and plan of the curriculum of religious education would exceed the limits of this discussion. One important feature, however, may be mentioned—that of the mechanical form in which curriculum materials for the church schools are issued. Partly as a matter of tradition and partly as a matter of supposed economy the materials are quite commonly issued in pamphlet or leaflet form for both teachers and pupils.

This is a serious educational error. The value of truth is influenced by the form in which it is printed and bound. Religious materials coming to the pupil in the form of temporary unbound leaflets, often inferior in paper, illustrations, type, and general impression to the advertising pamphlets that flood our mails and immediately find their way to our wastebaskets, cannot have the effect that these same lessons would have in the form of attractive textbooks.

Nor is there any incentive to keep this leaflet material as a permanent part of a growing personal library, so we seldom find any evidence in the home of the child's church-school curriculum. In fact, most of what is given out to children is mislaid, lost, or destroyed without ever having been used. Religious material should not suffer in comparison with public-school texts in the matter of attractiveness of form.

Nor is it at all certain that the temporary form of publication is cheaper in the end; in fact, it is beyond question a highly expensive and uneconomical method of issuing lesson materials. It will be granted, of course, that for younger children various leaflets, pictures, etc., are essential. For those old enough to read, however, a textbook system would be more economical based on the amount of use to be had from any single unit of printed materials. The church should *own* its textbooks and loan them out as the public-school district does to its pupils. If the pupil desires to buy the book and have it for his own, he may do so in either case. If he loses a book or injures it, he is expected to pay for it in one case as in the other. In this way successive classes can use the same texts for several years, thus requiring in the end much less of actual printing and distributing of material than under the present system.

CHAPTER VIII

THE NEW PROGRAM

It is evident even to the casual observer that a new type of educational program is developing among the Protestant Churches of this country. Every denomination is without exception recently seeking to strengthen its educational organization and perfect its educational agencies. Almost every individual church has felt the urge of this movement and is responding in accordance with whatever of vision and leadership it may possess.

The new program of religious education will not only call for new methods but for a certain amount of new organization as well. It is, of course, good economy and also good policy to use existent organizations in so far as they will serve the purpose. Wherever a new organization is needed, however, the church should not hesitate to effect such change as may be required. Nothing should be retained merely because it is old, nothing should be accepted just because it is new. The test of practical working efficiency should govern.

MAKING THE SUNDAY SCHOOL A CHILDREN'S CHURCH

Historically, the Sunday school is at the center of religious education in the church and will probably remain so for the near future at least without fundamental reconstruction. However, the present type of Sunday school could greatly add to its efficiency by certain changes in its organization, policy, and standards.

Out of the Sunday school should be made the *children's church*. The adult church can never successfully serve as a church for the children just because they *are* children with the requirements of children instead of adults. The church that serves the children must be primarily a *teaching* church just as the church that serves the adults is primarily a preaching church.

The present-day Sunday school is hardly adequate as a children's church, though it could easily be made so. To make the Sunday school into a true church for the children the program could be organized on somewhat the following basis with whatever modifications might be necessary to adapt it to varying conditions:

The Junior Church (that is, the modified Sunday school) should consist of all children from the Beginners up to the age of thirteen or fourteen. It should meet before the Senior Church services, say at nine o'clock, and close at ten-fifteen or ten-thirty. The program should be a varied one, with frequent changes of activity suited to the various ages.

The first half hour should be devoted to the preparation of lessons—supervised study, directed activities or the carrying out of other assigned work. It is recognized by every Sunday-school worker at present that it is practically impossible to secure any real study and preparation of the lesson materials. Supervised study and directed activities are provided for in the best public schools of the day and they are doubly needed in religious education.

The second period should be for general congregational assembly and worship. For this purpose the best part of the church should be used, the auditorium with its organ, architecture, and all other environmental influences capable of making religious impressions. During this period the minister will preach to the children a sermon of from eight to ten minutes—a sermon that has had as much thought and care in its preparation as the one intended for adults. The program will include much singing of children's hymns led by one who knows how to teach children to sing. The children will participate in short ritual responses and in congregational prayers. Every part of the exercises will be pleasant and enjoyable and devotional in the best sense. Adults may come to the service, but they must sit at the rear or in the galleries, leaving the body of the church and its best seats for the children. The teachers will, of course, be distributed among the children's congregation by classes.

During the third period the children will again meet by classes for recitation of the lessons prepared during the first period, for drills, dramatizations, discussion, expressional assignments and reports, for study assignments and whatever else is suitable to age and subject matter.

It is, of course, not essential to the plan that the three periods shall follow in just the order here suggested. But it is necessary that the three lines of activity shall be carried out; namely, *study, worship, instruction.*

The Junior Church should provide for definite recognition of membership, for promotion from class to class and finally for graduation into the Senior Church and church school. The annual graduation exercises should be celebrated fittingly. Children who have not prior to this time become members of the general church would then be received into membership. For those already members an impressive recognition service would be provided. By this method of close bridging over a great leakage from the church could be cured.

Some may object that the plan here proposed will break up the family and not bring the whole family group together at any church service. Two answers may be given to this problem: *First*, it is the rare exception rather than the rule now to find the entire family together at the church service, nor is the tendency growing in that direction. *Second*, except as a matter of sentiment it is not at all certain that the best religious results can be obtained by having the family all together at any one service of the church, since when this occurs one part of the family (practically always the children) are left unprovided for in the program of services.

Others may object that the plan offered is nothing, after all, but the present Sunday school somewhat modified. Precisely. The plan differs from the Sunday school only in the expansion and richness of its program and functions. It provides for actual study and preparation under direction; it seeks to introduce a serious, carefully planned, impressive program of worship; it brings the minister in contact as preacher with the children of the church; it recognizes and brings children to recognize a church for the children as well as a church for the adults; it provides for formal taking over of children from the junior into the senior, or general, church.

The Junior Church plan will, however, not solve the whole problem—at least as the problem now exists. For the curve of attendance in the Sunday school drops sharply in the teen age. Especially the boys of the high-school period do not go in large numbers to the church school, nor do the girls go as well as in the earlier grades. This is a fatal weakness, for probably at no time does the individual more need the stimulus and guidance of religious instruction than during the time of the difficult transition from childhood and youth to manhood and womanhood. Now is the time when ideals are taking definite and practical form. Plans are shaping for life-work. New temptations thrust themselves forward. Held to the church and its influences now, the life is reasonably safe; separated at this juncture from the church, there is danger of growing indifference and final disregard.

In every way possible, therefore, the church should strengthen this section of its school. The curriculum now offered for the high-school age needs radical and effective revision. Inspiring teachers who know and love the adolescent and who are highly skilled in materials and method should be provided. Good classrooms should be made available, teaching equipment supplied, and everything else done which wisdom and trained leadership can suggest to hold the young people in contact with the Sunday school and the church. For at this age they are no longer *sent*. They *come* or stay away. And they will come only if their interest and their sense of values are satisfied with the results.

Wholly aside from questions of organization such as we have been discussing, the Sunday school should seek to standardize its work on an educational basis. The educational survey has become an important instrument for improving public-school systems. For use in making such surveys there have been developed various scales, tests, and schedules by means of which to measure the teaching, curriculum, organization, administration, equipment, etc. A beginning in this direction has been made in the field of religious education, but much needs to be done.

It is possible, for example, for a public school system to say after such a survey: Our teaching force, based on standards obtaining in American schools, ranks ninety per cent in efficiency; our results in arithmetic one hundred and ten per cent; our language and reading eighty-five per cent; our buildings and equipment seventy per cent; our care of health and teaching of hygiene seventy-five per cent. Similarly, it would be a great help if each Sunday school could be able to rate itself on various aspects of its work by use of accepted standards applied to church schools. It might cure many schools of an unwarranted complacency.

THE VACATION CHURCH DAY SCHOOL

A new movement has grown up within the last decade for using a part of the child's summer vacation time for religious instruction. The public school claims only about three-fourths of the child's year for general education. While it is true that the child should have some free time for vacation, it is not necessary nor desirable that there should be three months each year of idleness. Indeed, after the first two or three weeks of the long summer vacation most children do not know quite what to do with themselves and gladly welcome an interesting program, a part of which may be instructional.

The movement for the church vacation school has developed so rapidly that literally hundreds of churches and communities have now come to use from four to six weeks of the summer for special schools organized for the children. The program is usually five days each week covering from two to three hours in the forenoon.

As in the case of all new movements there has been evidence of some lack of definiteness of aim and of method in connection with many of the church vacation schools. Some have attempted to do little except to bring the children in from the streets and amuse them for an hour or two in a good environment. Others of the schools have undertaken to base their program largely upon craft work of various sorts. Still others have worked out a better balanced program and use a reasonable portion of the time for serious and definite religious instruction while at the same time remembering to provide sufficient recreation and fun to attract this side of the child's nature.

Certain general principles, which grow out of the needs of the child himself, are clear with reference to the program of the vacation school. *First*, this is a *vacation* school and must therefore be somewhat different from the regular school of the work-time year. *Second*, the fourfold nature of the child should be ministered to: (1) the *physical*, in its health, cleanliness, purity, and general well-being; (2) the *mental*, in its requirement for interesting fact, discovery, thought, learning; (3) the *social*, with its comradeship, service, recreation, fun; (4) the *spiritual*, with its growth in religious knowledge and understanding, its training in worship, its carrying instruction over into character through expressional activities and practical projects of helpfulness and cooperation. All four of these needs should be represented in the curriculum of the vacation church school.

In general, it may be said that for the church, hampered as it is for adequate time in which to teach the child religion, this vacation time which commonly goes to waste is too precious to overlook or neglect. An important part of the modern plan of religious education will therefore be to organize and conduct an effective church vacation school, the length of which should probably be from five to six weeks. This may be done by individual churches but probably best by federated or community effort where conditions will permit.

THE WEEK-DAY CHURCH SCHOOL

One of the most recent and promising movements in religious education is that of the week-day church school.

Throughout all its history it has been the policy of the Catholic Church to combine religious instruction with general education. In order to accomplish this purpose, as already indicated, Catholics in this country have quite generally desired to draw their children out from the public schools and send them to parochial schools run by the church. In these schools religion has a regular part on each day's program as much as arithmetic or geography. As was said earlier in the discussion, this thorough instruction in religion from childhood up is no doubt the chief factor in the ability of the Catholic Church to maintain itself.

The Jewish people in the United States have also carried on a more-or-less effective program of religious instruction for their children. This has differed from the policy of the Catholics, however, in that they have not taken their children out of the public schools in order to give them religious instruction on week days. Their usual method has been to claim the time of the child for one class period each day of the week for religious instruction in addition to his regular public school work. In this way the Jews have, while remaining loyal supporters to the public schools, at the same time made sure that their children were not lacking in the fundamental knowledge and training of their religion.

With the Protestant Church the problem has been somewhat different than in either of the two cases cited. In the earlier history of this country the curriculum of general education was distinctly religious. The old New England Primer used for more than one hundred and fifty years as the child's sole introduction to reading and literature consisted almost wholly of distinctly religious material. The Bible was also regularly read and studied in the schools, as it was in the homes. Other religious books also formed a part of the school curriculum.

With the growth of the principle of the separation of church and state, however, the curriculum of public education was naturally secularized and religion dropped out of the public-school course. Along with this change the church home seemed to lose much of its interest in instructing the child in religion. The result has been that the Protestant child has for the most part little or no religious instruction except that received in the Sunday school and in occasional attendance at the general church sessions. This is to say that religion has been almost wholly lost out of his education and hence out of his general life equipment.

Two principles will serve to determine the amount of time which any subject should have in the child's general scheme of education: (1) *the importance of that subject in the life of the individual and in the welfare of society;* (2) *the scope, breadth, or amount of material in the subject necessary to be covered* in order to master it and secure its advantages.

Now, no one who believes at all in religion will be likely to say that it is of less importance in the life of an individual or society than any one of the public school subjects. Yet the child in the average public school of the United States will during most of the eight grades of the elementary school have from fifty to sixty hours a year upon the subject of arithmatics. At the same time this child, even if he attends Sunday school, is quite certain not to have more than six to ten hours of religious instruction during a year, and this under very unfavorable conditions. The result is that our children are not educated in religion as they are in the subjects of their public-school course.

Upon such principles and reasoning the church is recently coming to ask for a division of public school time in order that the child may have a reasonable proportion of week-day time for instruction in religion. The time allowed on Sunday does not afford sufficient opportunity to give the basic instruction and training in religion which the child needs. The addition of, say, two class periods a week, to the church school time, would afford a reasonable division of the child's entire educational time and still not cripple the program of general education.

Besides the securing of more time by the introduction of week-day classes in religion this system affords the advantage of giving religious instruction on somewhat the same basis as that which obtains for general education. The child in the week-day class in religion is more likely to employ there the same standards of study, mastery, and recitation that obtain in the public school than he is in his Sunday-school work. Furthermore, the very fact of carrying religion over into the week-day life tends to develop in the child the fundamental understanding that religion is not a matter for Sundays only but that it belongs in all relations and activities of living all the days of the week.

Some have feared that the extending of instruction in religion over into week-day time will again introduce religion into the public schools, which is, of course, not the case. The principle of separation of church and state is so thoroughly established in this country that it is no longer open to discussion. Those who are advocating week-day instruction in religion are not advising that this instruction be given in public schools, or by public-school teachers, or under the supervision of public-school authorities. These three fundamental tests define beyond question the responsibility of the church for its week-day schools:

(1) Week-day religious instruction is supported by *church funds* and not by *public funds*.

(2) The *curriculum* taught in the week-day church

school is selected not by public school authority but by church authority.

(3) The *teachers* and their requirements are determined, not by public school, but by church authority.

Once these three principles are definitely settled, there can be no question of combining religious instruction with public-school instruction or of stirring up the old controversy of the relations of church and state. The public schools do not desire to be commissioned with responsibility for teaching religion nor do the churches desire them to be delegated with this responsibility.

While week-day religious instruction presents many difficult problems, it is doubtful whether the church can do its duty in educating the child in religion without claiming some portion of his week-day time. Important experiments are now under way in week-day church schools, and many new enterprises are organizing. Toward the solution of this question the church should devote its best energies.

THE TEACHER TRAINING SCHOOL

No system of church schools is complete that does not definitely provide for the training of teachers of religion. It is an inspiring thought that we have in the United States nearly two million Sunday-school teachers and officers freely serving the educational program of the church without monetary compensation.

Yet in the very fact of unpaid service there is danger. The state is able, because it pays the salaries of the public-school teachers, to set certain standards for their education and make certain requirements for continued growth and professional advancement after they begin service. In the volunteer system of church-school teaching there can, of course, be no such thing as examinations and certificates and required study. It is doubtful whether the great army of church school teachers could pass a very high examination on the subject matter they are supposed to teach. The sense of duty, devotion and opportunity must be appealed to in each teacher to insure as full a preparation and growth as may be.

In every Sunday school of fair size there should be one normal class consisting of the most promising young people of both sexes who are willing to prepare for teaching positions as they offer.

For teachers and officers already in service the church and the community training school have been devised. Many churches now have special evening classes for teachers meeting once each week for from twelve to twenty-four weeks a year. Supplementing these and usually altogether stronger and more efficient are the community training schools consisting of workers from all the various denominations organized in special classes under highly trained instructors.

Both types of teacher-training schools are on the increase, but as yet a pitifully small proportion of our Sunday-school teachers have had or are taking any training adequately to prepare them for their great work. The church must train its teachers. It is as impossible to teach religion as it is arithmetic without knowing the materials or having mastered the technique of instruction. An irreligious teacher of science is no more of an anomaly than an unscientific teacher of religion.

THE HOME

Let us not conclude, however, that the new program of religious education can be carried out by the organizations of the church alone no matter how well the work may be done. *The home must do its share.*

Time was when the home was required to teach the child the rudiments of reading and number before he could be admitted to the public school. The records of the old New England town meetings contain many entries to the effect that "Goodman So-and-So is required to take his children out of the school until they have been properly prepared for admission."—that is, until the home had taught the beginnings of the "three R's." So also the old-time home taught the child in a very practical and concrete way what we now call manual training and domestic science—taught these things in the everyday routine of household duties in which every member from the youngest to the oldest had a responsible part. Now the home teaches practically none of these things. The school has for the most part taken them all over, and the home is relieved of responsibility.

In similar way the earlier home, the church home, taught its children religion. The family worship, the grace at meals, the Sunday readings of the Bible, the memorizing of verses, the learning of the catechism—these and other forms of religious instruction were a regular part of the family program, an accepted part of its responsibilities. But times have changed, and even the church family—the average family—seems to have handed instruction in religion over to the church as it has handed instruction in general education over to the school.

This will not work. No program of religion will work which leaves the home out. There is no possibility of giving all responsibility for religious instruction and impression over to the church as arithmetic may be given to the school.

In the first place it will not work because the religious impressions of the child should be begun earlier than the

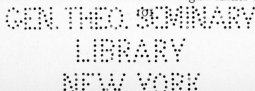

church can get him. Back of the time reached by the later memory the child should be under the influence of the mother's (and at the right time his own) bedtime prayer; of the quiet-hour talk and story; of the lullaby; of the grace said at meals; and of a home thoroughly permeated by a reverent religious atmosphere. For in these earliest years the most lasting impressions are made and the surest foundations laid. As the child comes to the age of understanding, the home can through the religious story, through simple talks and explanations by mother and father about God and about Jesus, through songs and hymns, and through direct instruction do more for the spiritual unfoldment of the child's nature than can possibly be done by the church.

Furthermore, after the church begins its training of the child there must be a laboratory for working out, making real, and putting into practice the teachings of the church school. The most natural and the best laboratory is the home. Here the lessons can be exemplified in the love and care and kindness of the members of the family. Here the instruction in obedience, in helpfulness, in truthfulness, and honor can find application and reinforcement—providing the home is in sympathetic contact with the church school and doing its share in carrying out the joint program of the child's religious training.

To bring the home to realize its share of responsibility for the child's education in religion and to help the home prepare to meet this responsibility is one of the first responsibilities of the church in its new program. Nor will it be sufficient for the preacher now and then to preach a sermon on the responsibility of the home, not even if he exhorts fathers and mothers warmly on the subject. He may do these things, but they are easily done—and not very effective.

The church should have training classes for parents just as for teachers. In these classes should be taught something of the religion of childhood, the way to begin to make religious impressions on the child, how to teach to pray, first ideas to give about God, how to lead to right observance of the Sabbath—such practical questions should be discussed by a leader who knows by experience and training how to meet these and similar problems and how to help parents meet them.

But the responsibility of the church does not end here. The home needs created for it and put into its hands a new literature on child religion. This literature must be scientifically based but wholly untechnical in form. It must not only discuss and illustrate methods but must supply an abundance of concrete materials in the way of Bible and other religious stories, songs, prayers, pictures, and whatever else can fruitfully be used in training the child.

It will then be the problem and the privilege of each local church, through every agency that can be brought to bear on the problem, to interest, instruct, train, inspire parents to use these materials in bringing the home effectively to do its part toward the religious development of its children.

A SELECTED LIST OF BOOKS, PAMPHLETS, AND ARTICLES BEARING ON THE PROBLEMS SET FORTH IN THIS BOOK:

Coe, G. A., *A Social Theory of Religious Education.*

Stout, J. E., *Organization and Administration of Religious Education.*
Week-day Religious Instruction.

Betts, G. H., *How to Teach Religion.*
The Curriculum of Religious Education.

Cope, H. F., *The School in the Modern Church.*
The Week-Day Church School.

Athearn, W. S., *Religious Education and American Democracy.*

Richardson, N. E., *Religious Education as a Vocation.*
(Editor) *American Home Series.*

Stafford, Hazel S., *The Church Vacation School.*

McKibben, F. M., *The Community Training School.*

Betts, A. F., *The Mother-Teacher of Religion.*

Crawford, L. W., *Vocations Within the Church.*

(The above books can be secured through your regular bookseller.)

McGiffert, A. C., "A Teaching Church," *Religious Education*, February, 1921.

Coe, G. A., "Religious Education Finding Itself," *School and Society*, January 20, 1915.

A SELECTED BIBLIOGRAPHY

Conrad, H. M., "The Lake Avenue (Rochester, New York) Plan of Religious Education," *Religious Education*, December, 1920.

Cowles, Mary K., "The Van Wert Plan of Week-Day Religious Instruction," *Religious Education*, February, 1920.

Seaman, W. G., "Gary's Week-Day Community School for Religious Education," *Religious Education*, October, 1918.

Squires, W. A., "The Week-Day Church School," Presbyterian Board of Publications, 1921.

Betts, G. H., "What Can Religious Education Do for the Church," *Religious Education*, June, 1920.

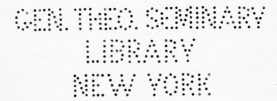

RELIGIOUS EDUCATION POSTERS

The following Posters and others on Religious Education
can be obtained in size suitable for wall use
from the publishers of this volume.

What Can Religious Education Do For the Church?

TAKE the Church back to the method used by Jesus and by the early Christian Church.

Double the Church's membership within the next decade.

Through conservation reduce the need for reclamation and multiply a hundred fold the effective outcome of funds and effort devoted to church work.

Vitalize and give dynamic force to the spiritual life of the Church by building religion firmly into the every-day character and experience of its people.

Provide for the Church an intelligent and loyal membership instructed in the Bible and trained in Christian living.

MAKE IT POSSIBLE FOR THE CHURCH TO TAKE THE OFFENSIVE FOR THE SPIRITUAL REGENERATION OF THE WORLD

What Shall the Church Do to Be Saved?

OBEY the great spiritual and biological law that one who would save his life must be ready to lose it in service.

Build its program around childhood. Change the center of emphasis from the adult to youth, claiming life at its source rather than reclaiming it at its end.

Awaken to the fact already discovered by the state—that education is the chief instrument by which it can fulfill its task and achieve its destiny. Build into the structure of young life the spiritual values necessary for its fulfillment.

Turn into its own channels the great spiritual stream of youthful energy and enthusiasm now going to waste in barren places for lack of religious education of childhood.

SAVE CHILDHOOD AND YOUTH THROUGH RELIGIOUS NURTURE AND EDUCATION

Religious Education The Birth-Right of the Child

The best and most natural way for the child to enter into his spiritual heritage is to grow into it gradually from the beginning.

Only those ideals which have been built into the structure of character from childhood later become a dynamic and dependable factor in the life.

New religious concepts offered a mature and hardened life are like fresh shoots grafted on old trees.

Spiritual ideals, loyalties, devotions and the consciousness of God in the life cannot come in a day. They are the products of wise, persistent training in religion through the plastic years.

No reclaimed life can ever be what would have been possible without the necessity for reclamation. It is always too late to be what we might have been.

Religion can and must be taught. In his religious development the child uses the same powers of mind and heart that are employed in other avenues of experience.

The new program of religious education does not substitute mere training for the Divine influence working on the life. It offers a way to prevent the soul of the child from ever breaking connections with the Divine.

Week-Day Religious Education

THE NEED:

EVERY American child has an inalienable right to a knowledge of the Bible and to training in the Christian religion.

The Public School can not teach religion; the Home increasingly does not.

The Sunday School is doing a remarkable work, but with its necessary limitations it can never fully meet the need.

We are in danger of becoming a nation of religious illiterates:

Children 6-12 years in U. S., 20,500,000
Children 6-12 years in Sunday School, 5,350,000

Two thirds of all American children receive no significant religious instruction.

Religion is as important and as much a part of life equipment as geography or arithmetic. Religion can be taught; it should have its share in any program of education.

Week-day religious education will help the Church meet this obligation. It is helping meet it now for thousands of children in many American communities.

LET THE CHURCH PUT THE CHILD AT THE CENTER OF ITS PROGRAM

Week-Day Religious Education

THE PLAN:

THE churches of each community should form a federation for the promotion of week-day religious instruction as a joint enterprise. Where this is impossible a single denomination should conduct the school.

The Week-Day Church School year should run parallel with public school year.

About two class periods a week should be given to religious instruction.

Classes are held in churches, or in public school or other suitable buildings as the community desires.

Time from school program is granted (on request of parent) for work in religion by public school authorities, or classes are held before or after school or on Saturdays.

Religious instruction is not to be a part of the public school system; teachers are selected, funds provided and curriculum determined by the *churches*.

Each church will maintain and strengthen its own Sunday School, which will be supplemented by the joint week-day instruction.

WORK IN THE CHURCH SCHOOL BROUGHT TO AS HIGH A STANDARD AS IN THE PUBLIC SCHOOL

Week-Day Religious Education

THE CURRICULUM:

GRADED Volumes for every age from Beginners on through the High School and into the College.

A series of text books as carefully planned, as well adapted, printed, illustrated and bound as the texts used in the public schools.

Every lesson embodies the scientific principles of modern education, but without sacrificing religious warmth or spiritual dynamic.

On the one hand the texts supplement the work of the Sunday School; on the other they correlate in grading and content with the work of the public schools.

The materials are carefully tested and proved in actual class room use under skilled teaching and supervision.

The Bible supplies the core of subject matter, but nature, literature, and life are freely drawn upon.

Large place is given to suitable forms of expression work planned to make the lessons carry over into conduct, habits and character.

Both in their content and their pedagogical plan the texts are such as will make the teaching of religion a joy and its study a delight.

The volumes are interdenominational in the sense that they supply the great fundamentals of religious truth and basic virtues whose need and application are common to all denominations without reference to church or creed.

WHAT WE WOULD HAVE IN THE LIFE OF THE CHURCH WE MUST FIRST PUT IN ITS SCHOOLS

The Church Vacation Day School

WHY waste one fourth of the child's precious education time?
The program of the Public School leaves 20,000,000 children idle for three months each summer.

Here is the Church's great opportunity. Through the Vacation Day School the Church can recruit its own ranks and Christianize the nation.

The long summer vacation is not only a period of wasted opportunity and retrogression but of grave moral danger to thousands of children. Save the danger by means of the Church Vacation School.

Let the Church bring together in the Vacation Day School the three anomalous factors: idle children, idle church buildings, and devoted but idle teachers.

Parents approve Vacation Schools, the children are enthusiastic over them, ministers count them one of the best agencies for the religious training of the young.

More than two thousand churches and communities have found in the long summer months an opportunity for supplementing the child's religious instruction and making fruitful use of his leisure time.

The busiest and most fruitful months should be the summer months for most churches. When the Public School closes its doors let the doors of the Church be open to every child.

**MORE TIME IS NEEDED FOR RELIGIOUS EDUCATION.
THAT TIME IS AVAILABLE IN THE SUMMER
VACATION. WILL THE CHURCH USE IT?**

The Church Vacation School Should

—minister to the whole child: physical, mental, social and moral: hence,

—provide instruction in the Bible.

—teach religion through nature, literature and life.

—make familiar the devotional music and art of the Church.

—broaden the social nature and quicken and enrich the sympathies by teaching the great missionary adventures of the Church.

—give lessons in Christian citizenship.

—build for physical well being, right habits, health and happiness.

—supply abundant recreation and give training in suitable games and play.

—afford opportunity for expression through the hand, social conduct and in such other ways as will lead to useful habits.

HELP THE CHURCH FULFILL ITS OBLIGATION TO CHILDHOOD

The Community Training School

Helps to Reunite Religion and Education

Solves the problem of supply teachers

Strengthens the morale of the teaching corps

Supplements the teacher-training programs of the local churches

Provides specialized courses of training

Creates reverence for the Word of God, for the child, and for the Church School

Exalts the teaching ministry of the church

Provides teachers with objectives, motives, skill

Answers the questions—who shall teach, how to teach, and what to teach

"STUDY TO SHOW THYSELF APPROVED OF GOD,
A WORKMAN THAT NEEDETH NOT TO BE
ASHAMED, RIGHTLY DIVIDING
THE WORD OF TRUTH"

II TIMOTHY, 2:15

The Community Training School

A poor teacher can spoil a good lesson

Are the pupils being taught or are they being merely sprayed with ideas?

Does the teacher of religion need less training than the teacher of arithmetic?

In teaching religion, religious motives are not a substitute for technical insight. Both are needed.

It is not so much—do you know how to teach the lesson? as, do you know how to teach the boy?

No person has a moral right to undertake to teach if ignorant of the subject matter or unappreciative of its true worth.

Which is worse—an irreligious teacher of science or an unscientific teacher of religion?

The Community Training School gets rid of both.

A NIGHT SCHOOL FOR THE TRAINING OF PRESENT AND PROSPECTIVE TEACHERS, PARENTS, LEADERS.